GOD'S BANKING SYSTEM

GOD'S BANKING SYSTEM

THE REWARDS OF INVESTING IN GOD'S KINGDOM

by Buddy Harrison

Harrison House
Tulsa, OK

06 05 04 03 02   10 9 8 7 6 5 4 3 2 1

God's Banking System:
The Rewards of Investing in God's Kingdom
ISBN 1-57794-418-6
Copyright © 2002 by Patsy G. Harrison
P.O. Box 35433
Tulsa, Oklahoma 74153-0443

Published by Harrison House, Inc.
P.O. Box 35035
Tulsa, Oklahoma 74153

CONTENTS

FOREWORD

by Jerry Savelle

Buddy Harrison was not only one of my dearest friends for more than twenty-five years, but he was also one of my mentors.

His keen insight and unique manner of sharing biblical truths was a tremendous blessing, not only to me personally but to thousands all over the world.

Many times he, Pastor Happy Caldwell, and I spent hours together discussing "the things of the kingdom," and Buddy would always have a nugget of truth that would amaze and inspire us.

His insights into *God's Banking System* blessed me then and still do to this very day. That is why I am so thrilled that this book has been published. Now you, the reader, have the wonderful privilege of gleaning from Buddy's wisdom.

As you read each page, I pray that the Holy Spirit will illuminate your spirit and give you greater comprehensive insight into God's plan for your financial destiny.

Thank God for men like Buddy Harrison who have shown us the way to God's best for our lives.

Sincerely,
Jerry Savelle

1

PROSPERITY

In 1765 John Adams wrote the following words in his "Dissertation on the Canon and Feudal Law":

> Liberty cannot be preserved without a general knowledge among the people, who have a right, from the frame of their nature, to knowledge, as their great Creator, who does nothing in vain, has given them understandings, and a desire to know; but besides this, they have a right, an indisputable, unalienable, indefeasible, divine right to that most dreaded and envied kind of knowledge; I mean, of the characters and conduct of their rulers.[1]

The founding fathers of this nation considered knowledge vital to the life and health of the Republic. In that sentiment, they were imitating their Creator: "Then said Jesus to those Jews which believed on him, If ye continue in my word, then are ye my disciples indeed; and ye shall know the truth, and the truth shall make you free" (John 8:31,32). Jesus said that knowing the truth, having an intimate knowledge and experience with the truth, makes one free.

One area where many Christians are not free is in their finances. They are bound by lack and debt. They may have enough to meet their needs, but they don't have enough left over for numerous and generous kind acts to others. They are not blessed; therefore, they cannot be a blessing. I believe they are in bondage for one of two reasons: one, they may not know the truth; or two, they are not acting on the truth they know. Either way they are in bondage.

Our heavenly Father told Abraham that He was Abraham's exceedingly great reward — El Shaddai, the lavish, extravagant, gift-giving God who is more than able and always willing to supply beyond our expectations.

Both the world and God have financial systems. When you invest money based upon the world's financial principles, you expect a return. However, the world's financial system is unstable, ever-changing, and often left to chance. When you operate in God's financial system and "put your money in His bank," you are depositing it where the thief can't steal and where moth and rust can't corrupt. (Matt. 6:20; Luke 12:33.) Therefore, God assures you of a tremendous return.

The Lord has called us to prosperity, not poverty. He has given us the power, favor, ability, and principles to obtain wealth. He has established a covenant with us and desires to prove Himself! If we aren't walking in the exceedingly abundant overflow, either we lack knowledge or we are refusing to act on the knowledge we have. I trust this book will fulfill its purpose to fill God's people with the knowledge of how to walk in the financial blessings God has provided.

Our discussion of God's banking system must begin with a basic understanding of biblical prosperity. Without it, we find it difficult to accept the need to operate and function within God's banking system.

In the beginning God created the heaven and the earth.

Genesis 1:1

Genesis 1:1 clearly tells us that God is the Creator. As the Creator or Inventor, God knows how His creation or invention should function, thereby making Him the expert. As Creator and Expert, God knows about prosperity: its functions and purposes.

We will never reach the fullness of what the Lord desires for us without understanding biblical prosperity. We may also pursue prosperity for the wrong reasons and travel off course.

God's prosperity has a purpose, and without knowledge you can miss much of what God wants to do for you and through you.

WHAT IS PROSPERITY?

And Joseph was brought down to Egypt; and Potiphar, an officer of Pharaoh, captain of the guard, an Egyptian, bought him of the hands of the Ishmeelites, which had brought him down thither.

And the Lord was with Joseph, and he was a prosperous man; and he was in the house of his master the Egyptian.

And his master saw that the Lord was with him, and that the Lord made all that he did to prosper in his hand.

Genesis 39:1-3

Notice that Joseph was prosperous. The *New King James Version* translates the word *prosperous* as "successful." Joseph was a slave, hardly a successful or prosperous person by worldly standards. Slaves own nothing. They are totally dependent upon their masters for everything, including their daily lives and what they are allowed to do. If the master provides food for them, they eat. If he doesn't, they don't eat. It's that simple.

So how could Joseph be called successful? The answer is found in the first five words of verse two: *the Lord* [Yahweh] *was with Joseph.* Joseph and the Lord had a relationship; they were friends. God gave Joseph the gifts, graces, abilities, and favor to ensure his success. He shared secrets (dreams, visions, and interpretations of them) with Joseph. The Lord was Joseph's protection and promotion. In the midst of slavery and imprisonment, the Lord was with Joseph.

Success and prosperity are possible for us because the Lord is with us. In our natural or worldly thinking, we equate success and prosperity with money, power, social status, and possessions. The biblical definition for success is obedience to God in the "small" things as well as the "big" things. We know from Matthew 25:21 that if we are faithful in small things, God makes us ruler over big things.

Biblical prosperity is not based on the amount of money, possessions, or real estate you have. It begins with your relationship with the Lord. If you are a born-again child of God, then the Lord is with you. Jesus told the disciples in John 14:23, "If a man love me, he will keep my words: and my Father will love him, and we will come unto him, and make our abode with him." We prove our devotion to the Lord by our obedience as we love Him and keep his Word; thus, the Lord — Father, Son, and Holy Spirit — makes His home in us.

Since God is with us, we are successful and prosperous. You may be thinking, *Sure, I'm prosperous all right. I'm living from paycheck to paycheck, barely making ends meet. I don't live in a fancy house, and my old car is leaking oil.*

That is what I call "stinkin' thinking," a wrong attitude, because you judge yourself and your circumstances by worldly, carnal standards. "Stinkin' thinking" is judging yourself and your circumstances with the wrong standard.

When you are in Christ, you are successful and prosperous. It doesn't matter where you live; the Lord is your protection and promotion. The reality of that success may not have manifested totally in the natural, but God sees you successful and prosperous. He sees you as seated in heavenly places in Christ Jesus. (Eph. 2:6.) The Lord sees you sitting with Jesus at His right hand where "there are pleasures for evermore" (Ps. 16:11). To see yourself that way, you have to eliminate wrong attitudes and thought patterns and begin to operate as the king and priest God has called you to be.

The key to success and prosperity begins with recognizing who we are in Christ. What is biblical prosperity, if it is not about the amount of money and possessions one has? Look at two passages of Scripture:

> **Now the Lord had said unto Abram, Get thee out of thy country, and from thy kindred, and from thy father's house, unto a land that I will shew thee:**

> And I will make of thee a great nation, and I will bless thee, and make thy name great; and thou shalt be a blessing:
>
> And I will bless them that bless thee, and curse him that curseth thee: and in thee shall all families of the earth be blessed.
>
> Genesis 12:1-3

The Lord spoke to Abram and told him to leave his country. Then He made Abram a great promise. Abram would become a great nation; He would bless Abram and make Abram a blessing. God promised all the families of the earth would be blessed through Abram.

The Lord didn't promise to only bless Abram. He promised to make Abram a blessing to others, and through Abram, all families of the earth would be blessed. We know Jesus ultimately fulfilled that prophecy. The blessings didn't stop with Abram, or even his immediate family. His blessings flowed to others.

God's purpose for prosperity is so that when He blesses you, you can be a blessing to others. Unless you bless others, you are not biblically prosperous.

> There is that scattereth, and yet increaseth; and there is that withholdeth more than is meet, but it tendeth to poverty. The liberal soul shall be made fat: and he that watereth shall be watered also himself. He that withholdeth corn, the people shall curse him: but blessing shall be upon the head of him that selleth it.
>
> Proverbs 11:24-26

Biblical prosperity is not based on mass accumulation. A person making $25,000 per year or even less can be prosperous if he is blessing others. Another person can make a million dollars every month, but he will not be prosperous until he blesses others. (Deut. 15:14; Luke 12:33; 1 Cor. 16:2.)

We see the Old Testament definition of prosperity is that God is with you and He has blessed you so you can bless others. This same definition of prosperity is found in the New Testament.

> **And God is able to make all grace abound toward you; that ye, always having all sufficiency in all things, may abound to every good work.**
>
> **2 Corinthians 9:8**

Notice the all-encompassing words in that passage: *all, always,* and *every.* That means nothing is left out. God is the beginning, the end, and everything in between. He is the all-encompassing God.

Here is Moffat's translation of the same passage. "God is able to bless you with an ample supply so that you'll have enough to meet any emergency of your own and ample besides for any kind act to others."[2]

God doesn't define prosperity by how much you have but by what you give. Jesus praised the widow woman for her giving. Though she gave only two mites, a very small amount of money, Jesus said she gave more than all the others because she gave all she had. (Mark 12:42-44; Luke 21:2-4.) The widow woman was a giver!

This is where you must change your thinking and your confession. If you are giving tithes and offerings, regardless of the amount you give, you are prosperous. If after you have given your tithes and paid all your bills, you have only one penny left over, you are prosperous because you can give that penny! Quit saying, "I'm poor," and start saying, "God is with me. I am His home. I am a tither. I'm a giver; therefore, I am successful and prosperous."

Meditate on 2 Corinthians 9:8 until it becomes part of your spirit. When your financial situation begins to look grim, read that passage and thank God you are prosperous. Write it down and post it all over your home. Do whatever you need to do to fully accept God's promise of prosperity.

It's more than meditating and saying the Scriptures. You must also tithe and give, but we will cover that part later. At this point, it's important to realize what biblical prosperity is and that you are already prosperous if you're acting on 2 Corinthians 9:8. Your success and prosperity are accomplished facts in heaven. It's time to appropriate it on earth.

God can supply you with money without a doubt. The world and all its fullness belong to Him. (Ps. 24:1.) Your lack is not about God, His ability, or His desire. He is more than willing and able. He told Abram He would bless him and make him a blessing. Through Jesus, as born-again children of God, we are the seed of Abraham and the children of the promise. (Rom 9:8.) Therefore, God blesses us and makes us a blessing if we will receive it and walk in it.

Since God can supply all the money you may need, the question is, can He get it through you? If you're not giving your tithes, offerings, and alms to the poor, God isn't going to bless you. It's not that the Lord doesn't love you or want to bless you, but you must choose to operate His way.

Remember, this chapter started by stating that the Lord is the expert in life and that His way is best. When you refuse to obey, you are saying that God's way is not the best way. You deny God and stop the flow of His blessings to you.

Biblical prosperity is having enough to meet your needs and plenty left over for blessing others.

KNOW GOD'S WILL FOR PROSPERITY

Beloved, I wish above all things that thou mayest prosper and be in health, even as thy soul prospereth.

3 John 2

The blessings of financial prosperity will only come to us as our soul — our mind, will, and emotions — prospers.

To come into the fullness of what God has for us, our minds must be renewed to the Word of God on a daily basis. (1 Cor. 2:6-16; Phil. 2:5.) With minds renewed, we are able to move into God's plan and understand His way and His purposes.

The goal of a Christian should be to agree with God's will. We can see from 3 John 2 that it is God's will for us to prosper in every area. John wrote that we would prosper and be in health. God is interested in the total man.

> **But seek ye first the kingdom of God, and his righteousness; and all these things shall be added unto you.**
>
> **Matthew 6:33**

Notice, God adds good things to our lives. He provides food, drink, clothing, and shelter. However, our priorities should be in order. We don't seek Him for things; we seek Him to know and obey Him, and to bring others into relationship with Him. He then takes care of the material goods on our behalf.

The Lord is the God of increase and abundance. He always deals with us on that basis. As I mentioned earlier, He told Abram, "I am thy shield, and thy exceeding great reward"

(Gen. 15:1). He declared that He was more than Abram would ever need.

God wants His people, His Church, to be dynamic and glorious.

> **So shall the king greatly desire thy beauty: for he is thy Lord; and worship thou him.**
>
> **And the daughter of Tyre shall be there with a gift; even the rich among the people shall intreat thy favour.**
>
> **The king's daughter is all glorious within: her clothing is of wrought gold.**
>
> **Psalm 45:11-13**

Jesus is the King of kings. We are the children of God. We can declare we are of God. As the verse says, "The king's daughter is all glorious within." The word *glorious* here means "weightiness, magnificence, wealth."[3] God is our all-sufficiency. Therefore, we can be weighed down with all that He is. That speaks of all His glory, and the fullness of it.

Too much of the time, we don't perceive God as interested in our prosperity. The following verse of Scripture establishes the will of the Lord.

> **Let them shout for joy, and be glad, that favour my righteous cause: yea, let them say continually, Let the Lord be magnified, which hath pleasure in the prosperity of his servant.**
>
> **Psalm 35:27**

12

This Scripture states clearly that God has pleasure in the prosperity, or success, of His servants. If prosperity were against God's will, He would have no pleasure on our behalf. It is God's will for His people to be prosperous and it gives Him pleasure. In fact, God gives us the ability to obtain wealth.

It is he that giveth thee power to get wealth....

Deuteronomy 8:18

The word *power* can also be translated "goods, host, might, riches, and strength."[4] In Deuteronomy 8, God warned the Israelites against complacency, self-conceit, arrogance, and self-sufficiency. Notice God didn't say *if* they prospered. He said when they prospered, they would be tempted to boast that their own abilities, power, and strength had made them wealthy.

God cautioned the Israelites to remember that everything they were and had, including their abilities, power, strength, and wealth, had come from Him. All goods or riches and the ability to get wealth came from Him.

The Lord is the giver of every good and perfect gift; therefore, wealth cannot be evil. (James 1:17.) It is only the perversion of wealth's use that is evil.

Possibly you are wondering how the translation "He gives riches or goods to get wealth" makes sense. Every seed reproduces after its own kind. (Gen. 1:11.) God will give us money so we can get money. It takes money to make money.

Christians often interpret the following passage of Scripture to say the Lord doesn't want people to be wealthy by using the argument that wealthy people can't enter the kingdom. That is not the point of the passage.

> **And when he was gone forth into the way, there came one running, and kneeled to him, and asked him, Good Master, what shall I do that I may inherit eternal life?**
>
> **And Jesus said unto him, Why callest thou me good? There is none good but one, that is, God.**
>
> **Thou knowest the commandments, Do not commit adultery, Do not kill, Do not steal, Do not bear false witness, Defraud not, Honour thy father and mother.**
>
> **And he answered and said unto him, Master, all these have I observed from my youth.**
>
> **Then Jesus beholding him loved him, and said unto him, One thing thou lackest: go thy way, sell whatsoever thou hast, and give to the poor, and thou shalt have treasure in heaven: and come, take up the cross, and follow me.**
>
> **And he was sad at that saying, and went away grieved: for he had great possessions.**
>
> **And Jesus looked round about, and saith unto his disciples, How hardly shall they that have riches enter into the kingdom of God!**
>
> **Mark 10:17-23**

This man whom Luke and Matthew call the rich young ruler wanted approval for his life, and he boasted that he had kept all the commandments. He believed eternal life was his reward for doing the right things.

However, Jesus always went to the heart of the problem. The young man may have appeared to have kept the outward commandments, but he had not inwardly kept the spirit of the law. Jesus' test of the young man demonstrated that eternal life comes by faith in the Lord. Good works are the result of one's love for the Lord.

God doesn't want just the "outward" man; He wants the whole man. This young ruler had set his affections on wealth, and in doing so had broken the first commandment: "And thou shalt love the Lord thy God with all thine heart, and with all thy soul, and with all thy might" (Deut. 6:5). He didn't have wealth; wealth had him. Giving is the cure for greed and stinginess.

Jesus merely pointed out, as He did in the Sermon on the Mount (Matt. 5:3) and the Sermon on the Plain (Luke 6:20), that wealthy people tend to put their trust in riches and forget God is their source; whereas poor people have only the Lord to trust.

In Mark 10:25 He essentially said, "Children, how hard is it for those who trust in riches to enter into the kingdom of God!" The problem is not riches but *trust* in the riches.

It may be difficult to be wealthy and trust in God, but Jesus went on to say, "With men it is impossible, but not with God: for with God all things are possible" (Mark 10:27). He was saying it is possible to be saved, love God, and have wealth.

Jesus did not sit in judgment of wealth or poverty. His only request has always been for wholehearted discipleship.

Since prosperity is equated with money, here are a few thoughts to consider about money before we move further into the subject of God's banking system.

MONEY'S VALUE

At the height of the Civil War, the Union struggled to pay its bills. With the war costing approximately a million dollars a day, the Union government was running out of money. So Samuel P. Chase, Secretary of the Treasury, came up with the idea of printing paper money to pay the Union's bills.

As the story goes, President Abraham Lincoln wasn't too excited about printing paper money, but the decision was made. Chase, being a devout, pious man, was insistent that the president establish a wise saying to print on the paper money. But Lincoln didn't want to be bothered by it and kept putting off a decision.

One day, Chase walked into a cabinet meeting. The president was sitting in his chair with his feet propped up on the table, something he usually did. Lincoln said to the assembled cabinet, "Well, if you are going to put a Biblical tag on the greenback, I would suggest that of Peter and John: 'Silver and gold have I none; but such as I have give I thee." In the ensuing laughter, the president withdrew to his office.[5]

This humorous anecdote about Lincoln is interesting because it shows how paper money printed at that time didn't represent real value, the same way paper money no longer represents real value today.

There was a time during the history of the United States when paper was printed as gold and silver certificates. These certificates were backed by the hard metals that had real value fixed by the government. The gold and silver were held by the government, a fixed amount of gold versus a fixed amount of currency. The paper money had real value and could be redeemed in gold or silver.

Today, due to legislation, money has only the value that is agreed upon by those who are involved in the exchange of money: the governments and the citizens of the countries involved. Therefore, we can no longer redeem the dollar bill for a dollar's worth of gold or silver. Money is only a tool.

Why do we pursue something that doesn't have a real or fixed value but only an agreed-upon value that can change daily? Today's dollar purchases a lot less than it did twenty years ago because its value has changed. Yet people continue to pursue money instead of God, who is eternally valuable.

God's value and the value of His Word never change. If we would seek first the kingdom of God and His righteousness (Matt. 6:33), then all these other things, including money, would be added unto us. Seeking God rather than seeking money is the scriptural way to obtain prosperity.

As we have already learned, prosperity isn't about the amount of money we have. Money is only a tool. It has always been a tool that simplifies interaction between God and man, and between man and man.

We should never pursue money, because it's only a tool with no intrinsic value. The Bible clearly tells us we should pursue wisdom.

> **Wisdom is the principal thing; therefore get wisdom: and with all thy getting get understanding.**
>
> **Proverbs 4:7**

It tells us plainly that we are to go after wisdom, and Jesus Christ is wisdom.

But of him are ye in Christ Jesus, who of God is made unto us wisdom, and righteousness, and sanctification, and redemption.

1 Corinthians 1:30

From the first page to the last, God continually tells us in the Bible that He is all we need. As we discussed, in Genesis 15:1 He refers to Himself as "thy exceeding great reward." And He tells us in Deuteronomy 8 that He gives us the power to get wealth.

First, we remember the Lord. We maintain a constant, daily communion with Him through prayer, worship, and His Word. In that intimate relationship, He supplies us with wisdom, and in that wisdom is the power to obtain wealth.

We must understand God's attitude toward prosperity, its purposes, how to obtain it, how to keep it, and our position of stewardship.

MONEY DEFINED

As long as we have lived and interacted with one another, money has existed in some form. There has always been a medium of exchange, something used to make payments and to account for debts and credits, as well as a way to calculate wealth.

The following list includes a few of the goods that have historically been used as money: amber, beads, cowries, drums, eggs, feathers, gongs, hoes, ivory, jade, kettles, leather, mats, nails, oxen, pigs, rice, salt, and thimbles.[6]

At one time a Roman soldier's wage was paid in salt. In fact, the word for *salary* comes from the Latin word for *salt.*[7] Salt is so common now that we wouldn't dare take it to the store to pay for our groceries. But in Roman times, salt was a valuable commodity and an agreed-upon medium of exchange.

The Bible tells us that Abram was very rich in livestock, silver, and gold. (Gen. 13:2.) Pharaoh gave Abram sheep, oxen, donkeys, camels, and servants. So we can see that Abram had both animals and precious metals to trade with others.

When Abraham needed a place to bury his wife, Sarah, he bought a field from Ephron for four hundred shekels of silver. (Gen. 23.) From this we can see that commerce, the exchange of goods and services, existed early in the history of man.

For most societies today, money consists of paper: property deeds, stocks and bonds, contracts, car titles, etc. With the advent of the computer and the worldwide web, there is electronic money.

What is the purpose of a medium of exchange? No one person can produce all that he needs. God gave each of us different skills and talents.

For example, I have managerial, administrative, and leadership skills. But I can't build a house or fix my car. If I need remodeling done, I hire someone because I don't have the expertise.

This differentiation of skills and labor is illustrated early in the Bible. Abel was a shepherd; Cain was a farmer. In Genesis 4, the Bible talks about Cain's descendants. Among them, Jabal was a herdsman; Jubal was a musician; Tubalcain was a forger of brass and iron items.

Since early times, people have traded to obtain what they needed. A woodchopper could trade an extra amount of wood for needed items, such as a cow, vegetables, or other necessities. A farmer often traded his surplus harvest for necessities.

When an individual produced more than he could use or barter, he would have to convert the extra to a form that wouldn't perish or lose value over time. In the past, transportation of produce, animals, or other goods was difficult. And what was valuable in one society wouldn't necessarily be valuable to another.

In his book *A History of Money,* author Glyn Davies cites an example that demonstrates the difficulty connected with bartering.

> It seems that in the 1800s a French opera singer performed a concert in the Society Islands. Her pay consisted of three pigs, twenty-three turkeys, forty-four chickens, five thousand coconuts, and considerable quantities of bananas, lemons, and oranges. Although this assortment of animals and fruit was worth some four thousand pre-1870 francs, it had little value to the opera singer, because she had no way to take it back to France or convert it into something more valuable to her.[8]

As society became more complex and personal needs increased, money replaced bartering for the most part.

In temple worship, the Jews were required to bring tithes and offerings to the temple in Jerusalem. When the first temple laws were enacted, the Jews were largely an agrarian society, so their tithes and offerings consisted mainly of food or animals.

Since not every Jew lived in Jerusalem, and because travel to Jerusalem was hazardous in many instances and refrigerated transportation had not yet been invented, the Jews could exchange their produce or animal offering for a form of money.

Once they had reached Jerusalem, they could purchase the necessary grain or animal offering with their form of money. This simplified their transportation problem and made it easier for them to worship the Lord with their tithes and offerings.

Without such a medium of exchange, a society will not function effectively or efficiently. So, money is neither good nor evil. It's simply a tool that enables us to interact with one another and with God.

Money doesn't have its own personality or moral value. It takes on the personality of its user. People, who are users of money, determine what happens with it. We can use money to bless others as God intends, or we can pervert its use.

Unsaved people and carnal Christians often try to use money to gain stature, prestige, power, and peace, but these qualities only come from God. Using money to obtain such things will merely frustrate and hurt those involved, and it could eventually destroy them.

Money, as a tool, represents your life. You have exchanged your time, talent, and energy for monetary compensation. Then, in turn, the money earned, if you are a wise Christian, is used to worship God and to take care of your needs. If

> *You would be mortgaging your eternity for the here and now.*

you aren't careful, you could sell yourself to obtain possessions. In effect, you would be mortgaging your eternity for
the here and now.

PROSPERITY ISN'T EVIL

Ezekiel 28 is an interesting passage of Scripture. By the law
of double reference, some theologians argue that this passage
refers to Lucifer, the angel who became the devil.

> Thou art the anointed cherub that covereth; and I have set
> thee so: thou wast upon the holy mountain of God; thou hast
> walked up and down in the midst of the stones of fire.
>
> Thou wast perfect in thy ways from the day that thou wast
> created, till iniquity was found in thee.
>
> By the multitude of thy merchandise they have filled the
> midst of thee with violence, and thou hast sinned: therefore I
> will cast thee as profane out of the mountain of God: and I
> will destroy thee, O covering cherub, from the midst of the
> stones of fire.
>
> Thine heart was lifted up because of thy beauty, thou hast
> corrupted thy wisdom by reason of thy brightness: I will cast
> thee to the ground, I will lay thee before kings, that they may
> behold thee.
>
> Thou hast defiled thy sanctuaries by the multitude of thine
> iniquities, by the iniquity of thy traffick; therefore will I bring
> forth a fire from the midst of thee, it shall devour thee, and I

**will bring thee to ashes upon the earth in the sight of all them
that behold thee.**

Ezekiel 28:14-18

Lucifer was cast out of heaven because he tried to gain
something that didn't belong to him. By trading his position as
the anointed cherub, he attempted to gain the favor, power,
prestige, and position of God. He peddled what God had given
him to become something he could never be. He perverted the
use of his position to bring attention to himself and attempted
to lift himself above God.

You can't use wealth or possessions to become something
you aren't. Money can't give you life or joy, for God is the
source of life and everything that pertains to life and godliness.
(2 Peter 1:3.)

The Lord is our Creator. We should never let the creation
become our source, for it's impossible for creation to satisfy the
longing that stems from our need for God. God will satisfy that
longing if we will let Him. As we recognize Him as our Source,
He will give us the wisdom to meet our needs in a godly, righteous manner. He will give us the power to get wealth, so we
can fulfill His purposes here on the earth.

2

THE PURPOSES
OF PROSPERITY

In the Gospels, Jesus shares thirty-five parables. One-third of them deal with money, wealth, or possessions. Therefore, due to the emphasis in Scripture, these subjects must be of some importance to us as believers.

Yet many times we have been misled. We haven't come into the fullness of what God has for us because we haven't understood His attitude about prosperity and His plan and purpose for it.

For years people have prospered strictly under natural laws. Some people have operated under spiritual laws and prospered to a degree. The ideal way to function is to observe laws from both realms, dealing with natural laws as well as spiritual laws. Both types of laws work.

We are spirit-beings, living in the natural. God wants us to move into a combination of these realms. Our obedience to both the natural and the spiritual laws will bring supernatural prosperity. We require an understanding of both so we can properly function in them. God is a God of order.

We know God is the Lord of the harvest. (Matt. 9:38.) We also know He is the Lord of increase and abundance. However, to fully allow Him to be Lord over everything as we should, we must open ourselves to His perspective.

Many people have the opportunity to prosper, but they miss out because when money arrives, they immediately spend it. Most of the time it is spent in their minds before they receive it.

When we receive money, before spending it, the first thing to do is pray. Then it is important to understand God's financial system so that it can work in our favor. When supernatural prosperity comes, it will be difficult to keep unless you understand God's purposes for it.

It's going to take money to finance the Second Coming of Christ. Jesus said that the gospel of the kingdom must be preached in all the world before He can return. (Matt. 24:14;

Mark 13:10.) "All the world" means that every nation and race of people need gospel witnesses, Christians who can lead people to Christ. (Rom. 10:14.) Going into all the world with the gospel takes money: money to send the preachers and missionaries to every tribe and nation; money to train pastors and raise up local churches; money to translate and print Bibles and other teaching materials; and money to broadcast the gospel via television and radio. Therefore, Christians need money to accomplish the great commission of reaching every nation, tongue, and tribe so that Jesus can return.

SIX PURPOSES OF PROSPERITY

Here are six reasons or purposes for godly prosperity:

1. We have dominion.

2. We are His stewards.

3. We keep His covenant.

4. We are blessed.

5. We bring honor to God.

6. We live in freedom.

When you discover God's purpose for your life, then make your plans accordingly. Remember, "In Him we live, and move, and have our being" (Acts 17:28). Take God's purpose, not just your own idea, and operate it in your life. Once that is done, circumstances and situations have a way of working out. You can live in safety and be steadfast. You don't have to be moved by the storms of life. Instead, you will be positioned properly, and God's blessings will be yours.

#1 DOMINION

And God said, Let us make man in our image, after our likeness: and let them have dominion over the fish of the sea, and over the fowl of the air, and over the cattle, and over all the earth, and over every creeping thing that creepeth upon the earth.

So God created man in his own image, in the image of God created he him; male and female created he them.

And God blessed them, and God said unto them, Be fruitful, and multiply, and replenish the earth, and subdue it: and have dominion over the fish of the sea, and over the fowl of the air, and over every living thing that moveth upon the earth.

Genesis 1:26-28

God created Adam for fellowship. Genesis 3:8 says God walked and talked with Adam in the cool of the day. And we are created in God's image, as verse 26 says, so we should exercise the same kind of dominion that God does. We have the ability to walk in dominion because He made us to be fruitful, to multiply, to replenish, and to subdue the earth.

God told Adam to have dominion over everything on the earth: the fish of the sea, the fowl of the air, the cattle, all the earth, and every *creeping* thing. That means God has given us authority over the devil! After all, the devil is the biggest creep there is.

One of the purposes of prosperity is to rule and reign in circumstances rather than allowing circumstances to rule and reign over us.

Today there are certain television networks, news reporters, and journalists who are obstructing the truth or withholding the facts in certain instances because Christians don't exercise dominion over those networks or print media.

When you own something, you have dominion over it. You can say when, where, and how your possessions are used. If a Christian owns a television network, he or she can refuse immoral and ungodly programming. But when a non-Christian owns the network, a Christian cannot determine the programming. The only authority the Christian has then is to turn off the television and refuse to allow the ungodly programming in the home. The more dominion you walk in, the greater your influence or power is in every situation. (Prov. 14:20; 19:4,6.)

Dominion is directly tied to the amount of money you have. Your dominion in your own home affects you and your family. Your dominion over an entire network or a major magazine potentially affects millions of people.

Remember Madalyn Murray O'Hair? One woman grabbed a hold of her dominion and authority, perverted it, and forced prayer out of public schools in the United States. She's a prime example of what happens when someone understands dominion and walks in it. Look what she accomplished without the Spirit and power of God. Think what Christians can accomplish when we understand the purpose of godly dominion and walk in it.

PROSPERITY HAS POWER

Some Christians have the attitude, "Well, if I make money, fine. And if I don't, fine." That attitude helps no one. The more money you have, the more dominion you can walk in, and the more influence you'll have. The Bible proves that in Eccelesiastes 9:16: "Then said I, Wisdom is better than strength: nevertheless the poor man's wisdom is despised, and his words are not heard." People in powerful and influential positions are not as likely to receive counsel from a poor man as they would from a wealthy man. Worldly people judge by appearances, unlike God who judges by the heart.

If you took a billion dollars to a third-world nation to build, equip, and staff schools, medical clinics, and orphanages, the government of that nation would listen to your counsel and allow you to operate. Your money would give you dominion, influence, and favor.

We have a cliché that says, "Money talks." Typically, that has a negative connotation, but money can "talk" for the gospel. My advice is to make every dime you can and give every dime you can. When you obey God's Word to give cheerfully, you walk in dominion and can subdue situations. (2 Corinthians 9:7,8.)

As Christians, we have been given a commission to go into all the world to preach the gospel, heal the sick, raise the dead, and cast out devils. (Mark 16:15-18.) It takes authority to do that. We must subdue the world and take the territory. It requires money to do that.

It is no secret that money has power. God wants His people to have the power to take dominion. Money gives dominion over the problems caused by war, natural disasters, and many diseases because it allows us to help those affected. After people's physical needs are met, they are more apt to listen to the gospel. Imagine what would have happened to the man who fell among thieves if the Samaritan had not had the money available to minister to his needs. (Luke 10:30-37.)

Money allows Christians to buy newspapers, radio, and television stations, and to form media organizations or entertainment companies that promote Judeo-Christian values. Money allows Christian publishers to translate and print Bibles and other Christian materials into every language of the world. Money sends preachers and Christian humanitarians around the world with the gospel. Prosperity enables Christians to take dominion over what was once the devil's kingdom.

Unless you understand that God's purpose for humanity is dominion, you will say, "Adam committed high treason. He sold it all and gave up his dominion." However, in Ephesians 1, the apostle Paul established God's purpose more clearly. His prayer in verses 16-23 demonstrates how man regained dominion.

Cease not to give thanks for you, making mention of you in my prayers;

That the God of our Lord Jesus Christ, the Father of glory, may give unto you the spirit of wisdom and revelation in the knowledge of him:

The eyes of your understanding being enlightened; that ye may know what is the hope of his calling, and what the riches of the glory of his inheritance in the saints,

And what is the exceeding greatness of his power to us-ward who believe, according to the working of his mighty power,

Which he wrought in Christ, when he raised him from the dead, and set him at his own right hand in the heavenly places,

Far above all principality, and power, and might, and dominion, and every name that is named, not only in this world, but also in that which is to come:

And hath put all things under his feet, and gave him to be the head over all things to the church,

Which is his body, the fulness of him that filleth all in all.

Ephesians 1:16-23

Jesus gave us back our dominion when He gave His life on the cross. We are to use prosperity to establish dominion in this earth.

#2 STEWARDSHIP

A steward manages goods, money, and property for another person. According to Scripture, God owns the earth.

Now therefore, if ye will obey my voice indeed, and keep my covenant, then ye shall be a peculiar treasure unto me above all people: for all the earth is mine.

Exodus 19:5

Notice God mentions the covenant. The key to understand is that the stewardship of all the earth is man's. Therefore, God has given us dominion over all His earth. He is the Owner; we are the stewards.

God wants us to exercise dominion, to take authority over the land, and to deal with the elements. Often we are waiting for someone else to do something when God is waiting on us to act. It's time to change our perspective.

The earth is the Lord's, and the fulness thereof; the world, and they that dwell therein.

Psalm 24:1

Since everything belongs to God, I'm not even my own. (1 Cor. 6:19,20.) If I'm not my own, when I go to work, I shouldn't be working for myself. Part of the reason some Christians aren't prospering and enjoying what they do is that they haven't realized they are working for God.

The silver is mine, and the gold is mine, saith the Lord of hosts.

Haggai 2:8

Psalm 24:1 says the earth and its fullness are His, and Haggai says the silver and gold are His as well. As Jesus says in Matthew 18:16, in the mouth of two or three witnesses, let every word be established.

As God's steward, you are expected to use and multiply what you are entrusted with. A steward does more than maintain the owner's goods, property, and money. A steward is expected to increase the value of the owner's assets.

God expects a return. The parables show you that He expects you to pay off His investment in you with your life and actions. The parable in Matthew 25 illustrates this principle.

Jesus told the parable of the lord who gave talents to his three servants and then left town. When the lord returned, he praised the two servants who had taken their talents and increased them. The lord was angry with the third servant because he failed to increase the amount he was given. He called him unprofitable.

The Lord expects us to increase the value of His assets. We achieve that by leading people to Christ and discipling them. Thus, His kingdom increases or multiplies. The better our stewardship of what He has given us, the more fruitful we should be in bringing people into His kingdom. The more prosperous we are, the better positioned we are to do just that.

The best image we have today of a steward is a banker or finance manager. He invests our money, and in return we expect increase. If our money doesn't increase under his supervision, we remove it from his care and take our investment elsewhere.

Some people don't have much because they haven't learned to be good stewards or managers of what they have been entrusted with. They refuse to take care of it and bring increase for Him, so He must give it to someone who will.

Your reaction might be, "But that isn't fair!"

Consider this: There is a divine law in the Word of God that states a simple truth. Jesus says we have to bear fruit; and if we don't, we will be cut off. (John 15:2.) This law works continually in the kingdom of God.

If you won't bring increase, then you are contrary to the very nature and life of God. God is constantly producing and providing increase. He's the Lord of increase, the Lord of abundance. You miss the entire nature of God if you don't grasp that He expects increase.

Another aspect of stewardship is that we prosper so we can leave an inheritance to our children and our children's children. (Prov. 13:22.) We are ensuring that the work of the gospel will continue by leaving our children and grandchildren an inheritance that is both spiritual and financial.

We are God's business partners and heirs to His kingdom.

And if children, then heirs; heirs of God, and joint-heirs with Christ; if so be that we suffer with him, that we may be also glorified together.

Romans 8:17

As an heir and business partner of his father, a son seeks to honor his father in the business and increase the wealth of the business. A son should have more care and concern for the family business than a typical employee or steward does. We have the responsibility to honor our Father and increase His kingdom as children and heirs of God.

I believe a son should build and bless the family name just as Jesus did.

LEARN HOW TO KEEP IT

And the Lord God took the man, and put him into the garden of Eden to dress it and to keep it.

Genesis 2:15

It's one thing to get something, and it's another thing to keep it. Many people can obtain money, but they can't keep it. An important aspect of stewardship is learning to increase and keep what has been obtained.

You must keep some money to maintain what you have. If things aren't properly maintained, you'll waste money on costly repairs that proper maintenance would have prevented. That's true for every area of your life, not just mechanical things. For example, preventive medicine is cheaper in the long run than waiting until serious symptoms manifest.

To keep money, you must know how to manage it. Money management has both natural and spiritual aspects. The natural aspects of money management are beyond the scope of this book. However, there are numerous excellent books on this subject, as well as organizations and schools that teach the natural side of money management or stewardship. I encourage you to study the Word of God and books about the natural aspects of money management. Both are needed.

Now let's look at the third purpose for prosperity.

#3 COVENANT

**But thou shalt remember the Lord thy God: for it is he
that giveth thee power to get wealth, that he may establish his
covenant which he sware unto thy fathers, as it is this day.**

Deuteronomy 8:18

Prosperity causes us to walk in our covenant with God. He made a covenant, and He wants us to keep it. God has already done His part. Now we must do our part.

> **The Lord did not set his love upon you, nor choose you, because ye were more in number than any people; for ye were the fewest of all people:**
>
> **But because the Lord loved you, and because he would keep the oath which he had sworn unto your fathers, hath the Lord brought you out with a mighty hand, and redeemed you out of the house of bondmen, from the hand of Pharaoh king of Egypt.**
>
> Deuteronomy 7:7,8

It is good to know that we have been delivered out of bondage. This is the Old Covenant parallel, but we are under the New Covenant, which is a better covenant.

> **Wherefore it shall come to pass, if ye hearken to these judgments, and keep, and do them, that the Lord thy God shall keep unto thee the covenant and the mercy which he sware unto thy fathers.**
>
> Deuteronomy 7:12

For some of us who have messed up, it's wonderful to know that His mercy is new every morning. (Lam. 3:22,23.) Even if we fall short, we will make it through because we still have a covenant with God and that covenant includes prosperity.

It seems there are few people in the world today who really understand the concept of covenant. A covenant is a bond that is not to be broken. It says, "No matter what happens, no matter what comes your way, I'm there for you. I'm going to stay with you through thick and thin. I will be there through the flood, hail, and turmoil. What is mine is yours, and what is yours is mine."

Prosperity is the result when we keep God's covenant. I'm so glad that He owns this whole world and the fullness thereof, because then there won't be any shortages. We have a full supply when we operate in the covenant of God.

As we walk in covenant with the Lord, we bring other people into relationship with Him. Believers who walk in covenant with the Lord attract the attention of unbelievers because a covenant relationship is a blessed relationship. As unbelievers ask questions, we are able to lead them to the Lord.

Another purpose of God's prosperity is to keep His covenant with you. He wants you prosperous and blessed. He wants you to help others come into His covenant and blessings.

#4 BLESSING

God wants to bless us.

> **Now the Lord had said unto Abram, Get thee out of thy country, and from thy kindred, and from thy father's house, unto a land that I will shew thee:**
>
> **And I will make of thee a great nation, and I will bless thee, and make thy name great; and thou shalt be a blessing:**
>
> **And I will bless them that bless thee, and curse him that curseth thee: and in thee shall all families of the earth be blessed.**
>
> **Genesis 12:1-3**

As I said previously, we are the seed of Abraham because of Jesus and what He did on the cross. Therefore, when God says, "I will make you a great nation," He is speaking to us. It is important to understand the family of God is a nation. There are blessings for us as a people which are not available to those without a relationship with God.

Bless means "to favor or endow with, to make happy and prosperous, to speak well of."[1] It is good to know that God speaks well of us and desires to bless and endow us with prosperity.

Universities receive endowments, which are assets (usually property or income) given by alumni.[2] The recipient then receives the benefits of that gift. So God wants to endow us with gifts.

When it comes to money, I think most Christians operate with a "Brill Cream" mentality; as the old TV commercial would say, "A little dab'll do ya." They limit God because they think they only need a little dab of money.

God wants us to operate with an understanding of endowment. He's ready to bless us, but we need to understand His purpose, His will, and His ways. We have to change our attitude, thinking, and perspective. Once we make the change according to God's Word, we will understand His purpose and plan, and we will position ourselves to walk in it.

As we understand His purpose and walk in His plan, we are changed into His likeness, into His image.

And I will make of thee a great nation, and I will bless thee, and make thy name great; and thou shalt be a blessing.

Genesis 12:2

When the Lord makes me a blessing, then I am His instrument through which His divine favor can flow to others, bringing them happiness, joy, and preventing misfortune in their lives.

I believe that being a Christian prevents misfortune in your life. It means you have eternal life in heaven, rather than in hell.

That surely prevents misfortune. By giving your money to feed the poor, you prevent the misfortune of starvation. Let me share a Bible illustration that's found in Luke 5. I believe it will help you to remember God's blessings.

One time when Jesus was preaching, He was pressed by the crowd. You know that Jesus' words were and are today life, light, and power. His words bless those who receive them, and this crowd needed to be able to hear what Jesus was saying. He looked around and saw a boat that He could use. Jesus said to Peter, the boat's owner, "I need to teach these people. Would you let me use your boat?" Peter agreed. When Jesus entered the boat, they pushed the boat out a little from the land, and Jesus was able to effectively minister to the crowd.

The Lord originally blessed Peter with a boat. By agreeing to lend his boat to the Lord, Peter helped Jesus preach to multitudes that day. His message changed lives, brought people joy and happiness, and prevented misfortune. Because Peter was blessed, he could be a blessing to others by bringing the Word of the Lord to them.

When Jesus finished with Peter's boat, He blessed Peter even more. Thus, Peter became an even greater blessing to the Lord as a disciple and ultimately a great blessing to all he personally ministered to, including all of us who read the Bible.

Prosperity blesses us and brings others into the knowledge of the Lord.

#5 HONOR GOD

God wants us to prosper so we can understand His ways and honor Him.

> **Trust in the Lord with all thine heart; and lean not unto thine own understanding.**
>
> **In all thy ways acknowledge him, and he shall direct thy paths.**
>
> **Be not wise in thine own eyes: fear the Lord, and depart from evil.**
>
> **It shall be health to thy navel, and marrow to thy bones.**
>
> **Honour the Lord with thy substance, and with the first-fruits of all thine increase:**
>
> **So shall thy barns be filled with plenty, and thy presses shall burst out with new wine.**
>
> **Proverbs 3:5-10**

Honor God by giving in faith. Proverbs 3:9 says, "Honour the Lord with thy substance." Immediately we think that means money, but money is only a part of it.

"Now faith is the substance of things hoped for, the evidence of things not seen" (Heb. 11:1).

To honor the Lord with our substance means we honor God by giving in faith. Many people who bring their firstfruits to God do so without honor to Him because they don't apply faith to it. They do it legalistically, out of the Law. When the offering bucket goes by, they put in their money and say, "There, take it." They aren't happy about it, and it becomes a gift without honor.

> Let them shout for joy, and be glad, that favour my righteous cause: yea, let them say continually, Let the Lord be magnified, which hath pleasure in the prosperity of his servant.
>
> And my tongue shall speak of thy righteousness and of thy praise all the day long.
>
> **Psalm 35:28**

"Shout for joy and be glad." That doesn't sound like someone who is unhappy, grudging, and hates to give to God. The people described in these verses take great joy in their fellowship with the Lord.

Verse 27 says, "Let the Lord be magnified." Magnification doesn't make something bigger. You can't make God bigger. He's already bigger than you or I could ever make Him. When you magnify Him, you see Him better.

The statements "to please God" (Heb. 11:6) and "the Lord hath pleasure" (Ps. 35:27) are very similar. When I honor the Lord with my substance and with the firstfruits of my increase,

I honor Him by giving in faith. I please Him, because He takes pleasure in my prosperity. If I honor Him and give to Him, He will make sure it is given back to me.

God has purposes, principles, and attitudes He wants us to observe. Remember His goodness. He has an overall plan for us to operate in. We bring honor to God when we remember His goodness. Remember Deuteronomy 8:18 says, "But thou shalt remember the Lord thy God...."

Remembrance is a memorial, and a memorial is meant to bring honor. When we remember God, we remember that He is the One who gives us what we have. Through remembrance, we honor Him.

#6 FREEDOM

God wants us to freely give out of a full heart. We make sure God is in our hearts by giving. As we give, we free ourselves from the world and move further into the things of God. This is how we walk in our dominion as God's stewards. God keeps His covenant and blesses us as we honor and remember Him. Prosperity brings us freedom to stop focusing on ourselves and our needs, and to use our faith to bless others.

Here is one biblical example of how prosperity freed a family from misfortune.

Now there cried a certain woman of the wives of the sons of the prophets unto Elisha, saying, Thy servant my husband is dead; and thou knowest that thy servant did fear the Lord: and the creditor is come to take unto him my two sons to be bondmen.

And Elisha said unto her, What shall I do for thee? tell me, what hast thou in the house? And she said, Thine handmaid hath not any thing in the house, save a pot of oil.

Then he said, Go, borrow thee vessels abroad of all thy neighbours, even empty vessels; borrow not a few.

And when thou art come in, thou shalt shut the door upon thee and upon thy sons, and shalt pour out into all those vessels, and thou shalt set aside that which is full.

So she went from him, and shut the door upon her and upon her sons, who brought the vessels to her; and she poured out.

And it came to pass, when the vessels were full, that she said unto her son, Bring me yet a vessel. And he said unto her, There is not a vessel more. And the oil stayed.

Then she came and told the man of God. And he said, Go, sell the oil, and pay thy debt, and live thou and thy children of the rest.

2 Kings 4:1-7

For some reason this widow woman and her two sons were in debt, and the creditor was going to sell the two boys into slavery to pay for their debts. No parent, particularly a mother, wants her children sold as slaves. The woman asked Elisha for help. His answer was to start a business. God supernaturally multiplied the oil. When the woman sold all the oil, she paid all debts and had enough left over to take care of them financially until such time as the boys could earn a living. Prosperity brought freedom from slavery to this family. The world's system to meet the creditor's demands was to sell the boys as slaves, but God had a much better system, and He still does to this day!

Let's now turn our attention to God's Banking System.

3

TITHES = CHECKING ACCOUNT

There is a system of banking in God's kingdom that runs parallel to the world's financial system. God's system is a spiritual one, and the world's system is created from the spiritual system. The world's system doesn't work as well as God's system because it is subject to the thief, while God's system isn't.

In God's banking system, there are three ways to make deposits into our heavenly accounts so that it is stored there for use in our time of need. God's system consists of tithes, offerings, and alms, or giving to the poor.

As you know, the world's system of banking involves the checking account, savings account, and loans. I parallel the two banking systems as follows:

God's System	vs.	The World's System
Tithes	=	Checking
Offerings	=	Savings
Alms	=	Loans

Tithes are similar to a regular checking account. As we receive financial income here on earth, we make a deposit into our checking account. Then we are able to live off the amount of finances made available to us. Tithes are designed by God to provide regular benefits to meet our daily needs as they arise.

Offerings, what we call freewill offerings or giving to the gospel, are like savings accounts. The reason we invest in a savings account here on earth is so that we can provide financially for the future. In our heavenly savings account, we deposit our offerings to God as a way of storing to provide for our future circumstances.

The third aspect of God's banking system involves alms, or giving to the poor, which I equate with lending. Proverbs 19:17 says, "He that hath pity upon the poor lendeth unto the Lord." Giving alms would parallel the earthly realm of banking that provides loans to individuals.

In this chapter I will focus on the tithe.

CHARACTERISTICS OF THE TITHE

The tithe has three main characteristics:

1. It's a tenth.

2. It's the first tenth, because God should always be first in your life.

3. It must be administered by someone else.

When it comes to tithes, you don't have to pray, "God, how much should I tithe?" The reason you don't have to pray is that tithe means "a tenth."[1] It is 10 percent of your income or your increase.

The tithe is the foundation of your financial success because you must give it first. The tithe provides protection for your finances and other possessions, and hope of a return on your offerings.

> Bring ye all the tithes into the storehouse, that there may be meat in mine house, and prove me now herewith, saith the Lord of hosts, if I will not open you the windows of heaven, and pour you out a blessing, that there shall not be room enough to receive it.
>
> And I will rebuke the devourer for your sakes, and he shall not destroy the fruits of your ground; neither shall your

vine cast her fruit before the time in the field, saith the Lord
of hosts.

Malachi 3:10,11

When we give the tithe, the Word of God says that we are
positioned to receive because the windows of heaven are
opened and a blessing is poured out; and we have protection
because the devourer cannot destroy the fruits of the ground or
the vine.

At this time, the Israelites were primarily an agricultural
society. If they lost their crops or herds, they lost their finances
and wealth. We can see that the tithe positions us to receive
increase and protects what we have. The tithe is foundational.
Your offerings aren't going to produce to their fullest potential
unless you tithe.

Don't argue or debate with God about giving your tithe.
Just do it. Don't develop a bad attitude or complain about it.
The Lord established the tithe for your provision and protection. You should shout and rejoice that He loves you so much
that He made a way for you to have increase and protection. He
takes care of you and insures your future.

A friend of mine is a missionary and humanitarian in
Zimbabwe. He started a vocational training school, a medical
clinic, and an orphanage, as well as a mother church. From that

mother church, his congregation has established smaller works in villages and in the bush.

In the early 90s a severe drought hit Zimbabwe. Virtually no rain fell until 1997. The rivers and creeks dried up. Most wells also dried up because they were hand dug and very shallow.

> *Protection and provision are the blessings and the benefits of the tithe.*

This man had taught his people to tithe. One of his pastors, who oversees a number of the smaller churches, was also a farmer. During the drought, this pastor continued to tithe. My friend reports that this pastor would regularly bring his tithe to the mother church. It would be a bag of grain, vegetables, or a goat, or occasionally money. When my friend questioned the pastor about his tithing, the pastor replied that God had told him to continue planting his crops and giving his tithe throughout the drought. During the entire five or six years of the drought, this pastor's well never ran dry, and his garden never failed to produce. Sometimes, his garden would have miraculous results, such as larger-than-normal tomatoes or more ears of corn to a stalk than normal.

All around this man, the crops and wells of his neighbors failed. When those people asked the pastor why his didn't fail, he cheerfully witnessed to them about God and His banking system! Protection and provision are the blessings and the benefits of the tithe.

Part of the reason people become upset with the tithe is that they give it last instead of first. Let me explain. Let's say you get your paycheck on Friday, and it's $400. First, you go to the bank and make a deposit in your checking account. Then you immediately write out a check to cover the monthly payment of your car loan. Next, you stop at the store and buy something you really wanted but not necessarily something you needed. Then you pick up some groceries and go home.

On Sunday, you go to church. Now, let's say after spending all that money, you have $60 left in your checking account. Ten percent of your $400 income means you have to write a check to your church for $40. But that's $40 out of only $60 you have left in your account. Then you start to cry, "God's taking two-thirds of my money! If I tithe, I'll have just $20 left in my account!"

What you should do is write your tithe check as soon as you get your paycheck. Every type of transaction with God has its rules and regulations. The tithe is no exception.

If you had paid the $40 tithe to begin with, you would have had $360 left in your account to do whatever you wanted. The order in which you do things affects your attitude. God should always be first. Take care of Him before you take care of yourself.

Your attitude when tithing is important. Scripture says that God loves a cheerful giver, one who is prompt and happy to do it. (2 Cor. 9:7 AMP.) The Greek word for cheerful in 2 Corinthians 9:7 is *hilaross,* and it means "merry, prompt, and willing."[2] *The Spirit Filled Life Bible* says that *hilaross* "describes a spirit of enjoyment in giving that sweeps away all restraints."[3] In fact, the English word *hilarious* is a transliteration of that Greek word.[4]

When I first began to pastor, the Lord instructed me to teach on giving tithes and offerings. One Sunday, when we received the tithes and offering, the congregation started clapping and praising God. Such a joy and excitement swept through the room. I was thrilled, and so was God because they were cheerful.

I have seen people dance, run, or shout when giving. It brings tears to my eyes and joy to my heart when I see that because I know they have taken a hold of the truth and all of heaven is rejoicing with them.

DON'T ROB GOD

Even from the days of your fathers ye are gone away from mine ordinances, and have not kept them. Return unto me, and

I will return unto you, saith the Lord of hosts. But ye said, Wherein shall we return?

Will a man rob God? Yet ye have robbed me. But ye say, Wherein have we robbed thee? In tithes and offerings.

Ye are cursed with a curse: for ye have robbed me, even this whole nation.

Bring ye all the tithes into the storehouse, that there may be meat in mine house, and prove me now herewith, saith the Lord of hosts, if I will not open you the windows of heaven, and pour you out a blessing, that there shall not be room enough to receive it.

And I will rebuke the devourer for your sakes, and he shall not destroy the fruits of your ground; neither shall your vine cast her fruit before the time in the field, saith the Lord of hosts.

And all nations shall call you blessed: for ye shall be a delightsome land, saith the Lord of hosts.

Your words have been stout against me, saith the Lord. Yet ye say, What have we spoken so much against thee?

Ye have said, It is vain to serve God: and what profit is it that we have kept his ordinance, and that we have walked mournfully before the Lord of hosts.

Malachi 3:7-14

God spoke to the Israelites, "Return to Me, and I will return to you." When the Israelites asked what they had done, God replied that they had not kept His ordinances. They had spoken against Him, saying that there was no profit in serving Him and keeping His law.

The Lord told them, "Ye have robbed Me." Israel indignantly replied, "Wherein have we robbed thee?"

God's answer was simple, "In tithes and offerings." We can rob God in two ways: when we fail to tithe and fail to give offerings, which include alms, giving to the poor.

In the natural, robbery occurs either by force or deceit. We cannot rob God by force. The Bible says God is so big that the heavens cannot contain Him. (1 Kings 8:27; 2 Chron. 2:6.) We could never make a cannon big enough to rob God. So we can't rob Him by force.

God is an all-knowing God. He knows the thoughts and intents of our hearts. (Heb. 4:12,13.) Nothing is hidden from Him. So we can't deceive Him; we only deceive ourselves by thinking we don't have to obey His Word.

We can't rob God by force. We can't rob Him by deceit. Yet, God says we can rob Him when we fail to tithe and give offerings according to God's rules. In what way do we rob God? We rob Him of His ability to bless us. If we don't do things God's way, He can't bless us. God must operate according to His Word.

Some people try to work out their own program on tithes and offerings. They decide when they will give and how much they will give. Then when it doesn't work for them, they get mad at God. The reason their tithes and offerings don't produce for them is that they aren't properly operating God's banking system.

Some people will say they tithe 15 percent of their income, but they don't. They tithe 10 percent and give 5 percent. I rejoice with them for investing 15 percent of their income into the work of the ministry. It's important to remember that the tithe is a tenth. I point this out because it has to do with the confession you make over your tithe and offerings. Unless you do it right, you won't get the full benefit of the deposits you make into your heavenly account. The tithe is the first tenth.

> *The tithe is one way of freeing us from selfishness and an ungodly spirit of control.*

The third characteristic of the tithe is that it must be administered by someone else. That means we can't tell the preacher how to spend the tithe, but we can tell him or her how to spend the offering.

For example, if your pastor receives a special offering to buy chairs for the sanctuary, that offering must be used to meet that need.

We can say how our offerings are to be spent, whether they go to missions, the building fund, radio or television, advertising, or an evangelistic outreach. Whenever an offering is specified, that is where it must go. But we have no right to tell the pastor how to spend the tithe because God is trying to free us of selfishness. As long as we can tell our pastor how to spend our tithes, we still have our greedy, sticky fingers on that money. If we haven't turned loose of it yet, then we still have it in our control. The tithe is one way of freeing us from selfishness and an ungodly spirit of control.

The Lord wants us to recognize that the minister is His representative. Hebrews 7:8 says, "And here men that die receive tithes; but there he receiveth them, of whom it is witnessed that he liveth."

When you give your tithe to the ministry or the church, it is a human being who receives that money here on earth. With your confession, God receives it in heaven. Though you are physically paying your tithe to the minister, you are spiritually giving to God. The minister is only the vessel or container that holds the money for God. He is God's representative who receives those finances, handles them, and manages them.

> *The tithe is the basis for your financial freedom.*

You say, "But what if he doesn't spend the money appropriately? What should we do?" We are to pray for him and mind our own business. That minister is under God's authority. We have no right to control him. If you think you do have the right to control the minister, you are saying, "I'm smarter and bigger than God."

Smart preachers place themselves under someone else's authority, as well. They should submit to another minister whom they respect, one who is mature in the Lord and who will counsel them as needed. However, the decision to do that is up to the minister.

The tithe is the basis for your financial freedom. It is God's avenue of provision and protection for you and everything that concerns you.

Just as God specifically tells us the tithe is 10 percent, He is specific in where He wants us to pay the tithe. Again, Malachi 3:10 says, "Bring ye all the tithes into the storehouse, that there may be meat in mine house, and prove me now herewith, saith the Lord of hosts, if I will not open you the windows of heaven, and pour you out a blessing, that there shall not be room enough to receive it."

God emphatically says to bring the tithes to the storehouse. In Bible times, the storehouse referred to in Malachi 3:10 is His temple.

> And it shall be, when thou art come in unto the land which
> the Lord thy God giveth thee for an inheritance, and possessest
> it, and dwellest therein;
>
> That thou shalt take of the first of all the fruit of the earth,
> which thou shalt bring of thy land that the Lord thy God giveth
> thee, and shalt put it in a basket, and shalt go unto the place
> which the Lord thy God shall choose to place his name there.
>
> And thou shalt go unto the priest that shall be in those
> days, and say unto him, I profess this day unto the Lord thy
> God, that I am come unto the country which the Lord sware
> unto our fathers for to give us.
>
> And the priest shall take the basket out of thine hand, and
> set it down before the altar of the Lord thy God.
>
> Deuteronomy 26:1-4

God told the Israelites to bring their tithes and firstfruits to the place where His name dwells. Eventually, that place was the temple in Jerusalem, where the priests offered the sacrifices and ministered to the Lord.

The Israelites were to bring their tithes and offerings to the temple so there would be meat, things to offer to God and food for the priests to eat, in God's house.

Today, we know that all Christians are the temple of the Lord. God no longer dwells in a house made with hands. Our storehouse today is the place where we receive our spiritual food and fulfill our gospel commission. For most of the body of Christ, that place is their local church where they hear the Word preached, fellowship with believers, and do the work of the ministry.

Some people who attend a church think they should give their tithes to a missionary or television evangelist. If they are being fed in their local church, that is where they should give their tithes. If they are not being fed by that local church and fulfilling their gospel commission there, then they should find the place where they will be fed.

It may be that there is no church in their area that is preaching the full counsel of God, or that they cannot go to church due to physical problems. Then if a television preacher is feeding them, by all means they should send their tithes to that ministry. However, for the most part, the local church is where the tithe belongs, and offerings can be given to missionaries and television ministries.

I like to put it this way: If you eat at McDonald's, you don't pay at Dairy Queen. You pay where you eat.

SECRETS OF THE STOREHOUSE

Friends share secrets. Abraham was called a friend of God (James 2:23), and God shared secrets with him. He told

Abraham what was going to happen to Sodom and Gomorrah. (Gen. 18.) Abraham is called a friend of God because he believed God and acted on what God said. Abraham was a tither and a worshiper of God. (Gen. 14:20.)

Psalm 119:130 plainly tells us "The entrance of thy words giveth light; it giveth understanding unto the simple."

God's Word gives ideas and understanding. J.C. Penny founded his billion-dollar department store business on biblical ethics.[5] A tither who had a servant's heart, R.G. LeTourneau, allowed God to use him to invent the biggest, most powerful, and most productive earth-moving equipment of the twentieth century.[6] Robert Laidlow, a tither from his youth, started a successful mail-order business in New Zealand in 1909. By 1919, he was giving 50 percent of his earnings to the gospel.[7]

God gave these wonderful ideas to men who worshiped Him and fellowshipped with Him. I like to call them secrets of the storehouse. And God has many more secrets in His storehouse for those who will worship Him with their tithes!

Once while working for Kenneth Hagin Ministries, I found myself faced with a perplexing problem. One of the duties I handled for Brother Hagin was the operation of the prayer room. In his meetings, he would give an altar call for people to be saved, be filled with the Holy Spirit, and come back into fellowship with God. My job was to counsel and give them some spiritual help and direction. In order to do that, I wanted to put something into their hands that they could take home for further study. There wasn't anything available that satisfied that longing in my heart, yet I didn't know what to do about it.

I had been paying my tithes, worshiping, and fellowshipping with the Lord, and as I was driving down the road, crying out to Him, the Holy Spirit suddenly spoke to me. He said, *I want you to put out three minibooks. The first one is to be printed in green, and it will be called* The New Birth. *Put these Scriptures in it. The second one will be on the Holy Spirit and it will be printed in red to give people the fire of the Holy Ghost. It will be titled* Why Tongues? *The third book will be printed in blue, and in it will be all the Scriptures that include the phrase 'in him.' You will call it* In Him. *That will help those who have been in and out of fellowship. It will stabilize them. When you have done those booklets, you will then have something to leave in the hands of the people.*

That one idea given to me by God that day resulted in the publication of some of Brother Hagin's greatest books. God gave me an idea.

I picked up on the mind of Christ because I am a tither and worshiper. Therefore, I had a right to expect the windows of heaven to be opened to me and for me to receive the secrets of the storehouse. That is exactly what happened. Suddenly, coming down upon me from heaven, was an idea that stirred within me and provided the answer to the problem that I had been struggling with for weeks. Just one secret from the storehouse solved my problem and has blessed thousands and thousands of people to this day.

Tithes were paid before the Law. I have heard people say, "I've been redeemed from the curse of the law, so I don't have to tithe. That was under the Old Covenant." Unfortunately, those people don't realize that the tithe was in operation long before the Law was given. It continued in operation during the Law, and it continues now because it is a principle found all through the Word of God. The only reason it was tied into the Law is that it had promise of blessing with it.

The tithe goes back to the Garden of Eden. Adam and Eve could partake of the fruit of all the other trees in the Garden, except the Tree of the Knowledge of Good and Evil. That tree served as a reminder that God is the Creator and Owner of all. The tithe reminds us of our position with God. He's the Creator; we're the created.

By designating that tree for Himself, God was saying to Adam, "All this is Mine. I'm putting you here to dress it and to keep it. You're the steward. I'm the Owner."

After Adam and Eve were expelled from the Garden, they had children. Their children, Cain and Abel, brought their first-fruits to the Lord. (Gen. 4:3,4.)

Genesis 14 records Abraham's giving the tithe.

> **And Melchizedek king of Salem brought forth bread and wine: and he was the priest of the most high God.**
>
> **And he blessed him, and said, Blessed be Abram of the most high God, possessor of heaven and earth:**
>
> **And blessed be the most high God, which hath delivered thine enemies into thy hand. And he gave him tithes of all.**
>
> **Genesis 14:18-20**

Abraham must have taught Isaac about tithing because Genesis records that Jacob, Isacc's son and Abraham's grandson, offered tithe to God. (Gen. 28:22.)

Tithing is not legalism, bondage, or part of the curse. It is God's provision for our financial freedom and His way of blessing us.

I have heard people say, "Well, Jesus never taught on paying tithes. He fulfilled the law, so I don't have to tithe." People who say things like that show that they haven't thoroughly studied the Bible.

First, you have to ask, "What law are you talking about? The law of gravity? The law of electricity? The Levitical law?"

There are certain laws the Lord set in operation from the beginning of creation that we are not redeemed from. They will work whether we believe in them or not. For example, you can jump out of a tree and confess, "I don't believe in gravity. I don't believe in gravity." You will still fall to the ground because the law of gravity works regardless of your belief.

Jesus fulfilled the Levitical law. He kept all of it perfectly in order to offer Himself as the sinless Lamb, the perfect sacrifice. Thus, He redeemed us from the curse of the law. Actually, He established a higher law for us to follow, the law of love. If we operate in love, we will tithe and give.

Jesus taught on the tithe in Matthew 23:23 and Luke 11:42.

> **Woe unto you, scribes and Pharisees, hypocrites! for ye pay tithe of mint and anise and cummin, and have omitted the weightier matters of the law, judgment, mercy, and faith: these ought ye to have done, and not to leave the other undone.**
>
> **Matthew 23:23**

> **But woe unto you, Pharisees! for ye tithe mint and rue and all manner of herbs, and pass over judgment and the love of God: these ought ye to have done, and not to leave the other undone.**
>
> **Luke 11:42**

Jesus was not condemning the Pharisees for paying tithe on the smallest of garden herbs. The Law required the tithe, but the Pharisees took the Law to the extreme. They were meticulous and scrupulous in the outward matters. They publicly displayed their religion but neglected God's demand for inner holiness, charity toward the poor, love, and mercy. Jesus said they should tithe—"these ought ye to have done"—but they shouldn't neglect love and justice. Paying the tithe is an accepted discipline of someone who loves God.

TITHE IS WORSHIP

Worshiping God is more than going to church and singing songs. The Bible clearly teaches that worship is a lifestyle, the way we should live every day.

> **I beseech you therefore, brethren, by the mercies of God, that ye present your bodies a living sacrifice, holy, acceptable unto God, which is your reasonable service.**
>
> **Romans 12:1**

"Reasonable service" can also be translated "spiritual act of worship" (NIV). What we do every day and how we do it is part of worship. I believe worship is any act or position taken that establishes the relative position of God and man.

Our increase, whether it is in the form of money or possessions, land, goods, crops, or herds, represents a portion of our lives. After all, we used our time, energy, and faith to obtain those things. Therefore, when we present our tithes, as well as our offerings, to God, we worship Him. Giving is part of our "reasonable service," or our "spiritual act of worship."

In Deuteronomy 28, Moses instructed the Israelites to make a confession to God when they brought their firstfruits and tithes to the priests in the temple. They were to thank God for His deliverance and provision, declare their obedience, and ask for His continued blessing.

In one sense, payment of the tithe is the highest form of worship because doing so declares the sovereignty of God. By sovereignty, I mean that the Lord is the Most High God, that He is imperial, the highest authority. When we bring the tithe to God, we declare that the Lord is the Most High God, the Possessor of heaven and earth, and the Deliverer from all our enemies. Presenting the tithe is just about the only act that can declare that. We can say that God is sovereign, but the action of paying the tithe proves that we believe what we have said.

> *The tithe is a declaration of your independence from the world's financial system.*

I trust you are beginning to see the tithe a little differently now. Tithing is not a matter of "God gets 10 percent and we get 90 percent." It is all His. With the 10 percent we return to the Lord, we worship Him, acknowledge that He is the Owner of it all, and that we are His stewards in this earth.

Our tithes are just as much worship unto God as praising Him with the fruit of our lips. We praise the Lord with our words for all His blessings that overtake us. Those blessings will come to pass if you have made deposits in your heavenly account.

The tithe is also a declaration of your independence from the world's financial system. Every time you drop your tithe into the offering, you should declare:

"This is my declaration of independence. I'm free from the world's system! I don't care if the stock market goes up or down, in or out. It doesn't matter to me. As a tither, I'm on God's financial plan. So, I'm telling the devil and the whole world that God is my Source."

Every time you tithe, you exclaim that God is alive. Your tithe reaffirms this fact and acknowledges that He is the Most High God, Creator of heaven and earth, and Deliverer out of the hand of every enemy. You state this each time you put your money into God's hands. The tithe is where the blessings start and is the most powerful aspect of God's banking system when you operate it as it was intended.

Provision and protection are your promises from God when you tithe. The windows of heaven are opened for the tither, and the devourer is rebuked. (Mal. 3:10,11.)

TITHING IS STEWARDSHIP

Tithing is stewardship in microcosm. By that I mean that tithing brings things down to their essence. Just as a microscope enlarges things, tithing reduces things. It takes something that is huge, the earth and the fullness thereof, and brings it down to a level and size where you and I can manage it.

As God's stewards, we are to manage the whole earth, because that is what God created man to do. He made the whole creation, and then He made man to be in charge of it for Him.

How are we going to exercise dominion and control over the oceans, the mines, the oil and gas fields, the farmlands, and everything else in this world today? The unsaved world is not doing it, so how in the world are we going to be able to manage all that?

That is why we have been given the tithe. It takes all those vast interests and reduces them down to something that is manageable. You and I cannot manage everything that is out there in this world, but we can manage the part of God's possessions that has been given to each of us.

The tithing Christian prospers.

73

When you and I take the 10 percent of what has been placed into our hands and present it to God, we are acting as wise stewards and managers of what God has given to us.

The tithing Christian prospers. It is not because he is smarter, shrewder, wiser, or a better businessperson than others, but because, like Abraham, he has a covenant with God. When he gives back to God a portion of God's possessions, he is blessed in what is left in his control.

I am prosperous, not because I am the world's best businessman or the greatest money manager that has ever lived but because I am a tither. Since I present my tithes to the Lord, I have set in motion a law that operates for me. My management of the 10 percent determines what happens to the other 90 percent left in my hands. And the law will work for you, as it has for me, when you learn to manage the tithe.

TITHING AND DOMINION

As you study the Bible, you can see that tithers have dominion. They walk in a level of blessing and authority that non-tithers don't have. You can see that in Abraham's life. Abraham always came out ahead in his dealings with others, even in war. You will remember from chapter two that one of the purposes of prosperity is dominion, and from this chapter you have learned that tithing is the foundation for your financial success. The tithe brings dominion.

Let me give you a modern-day example of tithing and dominion. An acquaintance of mine was the pastor of a church in upstate New York where IBM started. Several people in his church were executives in the IBM corporation.

One of the young men in this church stuttered terribly as a teenager. He had a difficult time expressing himself with words. Then he was saved and was filled with the Holy Spirit. When he began to pay his tithes, all his stuttering left him, and he could talk well. He furthered his education and went to work for IBM. He continued to grow and develop, advancing from position to position.

From New York, he was sent to Huntsville, Alabama, where he was involved with the computer aspects of the space program and became very knowledgeable. Then he was sent to the Houston area, which was a great promotion for him.

From Houston, he was transferred to Norway to one of the units that electronically monitor atomic explosions anywhere in the earth. He was in Norway for quite a while.

When he returned to the United States, he called on his pastor. One of the first things that his pastor noticed was that the man stuttered very badly again.

The young man asked his pastor, "Have you ever heard of the Peter Principle?" People in business know this principle says that a person is promoted to the level of his incompetence. As he continues to advance, sooner or later he gets to a place that is beyond his ability and mentality.

"Pastor, that's what has happened to me," this young man said. "I've finally been promoted to a point in the company where I'm beyond my abilities, mentally and physically and every way, so I'm stuttering again."

As the pastor listened to the young man, he was praying. Suddenly he said, "Now, son, let me ask you a question. Are you still giving your tithe unto God?"

The young man dropped his head and didn't say anything. Finally, he looked up at his pastor and said, "Well, to tell you the truth, no."

Then he went on to explain: "When I was in Norway, there were no English-speaking churches. I would go several miles away to the only church that was there. The service was in Norwegian, and I didn't get anything out of it. I got tired of going Sunday after Sunday, not understanding what was being said. I wasn't being fed; therefore, I quit presenting my tithe to the Lord. Now I have gotten this new promotion here in the States."

The company had brought this young man back to work in Washington, D.C., as head of security for IBM. The pastor looked at him and said, "Do you know what's wrong?"

"No, sir," he said. "That's why I came to you."

His pastor told him, "You lost your dominion when you stopped presenting your tithe to God." If you want to get it back, you have to ask God to forgive you right now and present your tithe unto the Lord again."

The pastor prayed with this young man, who then got out his checkbook, wrote a check, presented it to God, and went on his way.

Several months later the pastor received a phone call from this young man. As they talked, the pastor noticed that the young man no longer stuttered.

"I notice that you are not stuttering," he said.

"No, I'm not having a problem," he replied.

"Well, what about your new job? You felt like you had been promoted beyond your abilities and mentality."

"Oh, not anymore; the job is a snap."

This young man regained his dominion because he presented his tithes to the Lord again.

> *Wherever you put your money, that is where you'll focus all your time, energy, and attention.*

Tithing is directly related to your dominion. You can't control everything in the earth by your own means. You don't have the knowledge or capability to reach out and touch it.

However, you can control the money and possessions that God has given you. You can present your tithe to God and by so doing say to Him: "Lord, You are still in control." Thus, you are declaring His sovereignty and your stewardship of His possessions.

If you feel that you don't have any control or dominion, consider whether or not you are presenting your tithe to God.

THE TITHE AS A GUARD FOR YOUR HEART

According to Jesus, presenting your tithes to God keeps your heart in the right place:

> **But lay up for yourselves treasures in heaven, where neither moth nor rust doth corrupt, and where thieves do not break through nor steal: for where your treasure is, there will your heart be also.**
>
> **Matthew 6:20,21**

Jesus spoke very plainly here. He said that wherever you put your money, that is where you'll focus all your time, energy, and attention.

If you put all your money into your possessions, like your house or boat or car, then you aren't going to focus on meeting the needs of others. If you don't tithe, you won't focus on what God is doing and what He wants, because you'll be concerned about all your things. Consequently, you'll miss out on the fullness of God's blessings since you aren't interested in what He's interested in. If you want to keep your heart in the right place, tithe.

TITHING

Some people think that because they pay their tithes, God stands around waiting to rebuke the devil on their behalf. But that's an inaccurate portrayal.

There is a difference between the tithe and tithing. The tithe is the 10 percent you put into the ministry. Tithing is the confession you make with your mouth about that tithe. It is what you say about that 10 percent. According to Romans 10:10, we believe in our hearts and then we speak with our mouths what we believe. Many people have given their tithe, but they haven't done the tithing.

In the book of Leviticus, it teaches us when God's people began to worship with their tithes, they would come before the high priest of that day. We also saw this from the Scripture mentioned previously in Deuteronomy 26. Our High Priest today is Jesus. As you present your tithe, you should make your confession about your gift, stating what it will do on your behalf. You've got to give Jesus something to work with.

People who don't believe in tithing, confessing God's Word over their tithes, are just giving the tithe because it's required at their church. I have seen people like that who tithe and never receive a return. They pay their tithes, but they aren't tithing or confessing. When the offering plate goes by, they just throw their money in. They are what I would call "plunkers."

Plunkers say, "You know, it really doesn't do any good to tithe. I put my money in, but I don't see the benefit in it. I do it because I'm supposed to." They believe it doesn't really work for them. Doesn't that sound like what God said in Malachi 3 about the Israelites' words?

Jesus, our High Priest, goes before the Father and worships Him in our behalf. He presents that tithe to the Father and tells Him, "Father, Brother So-and-So says he gave his tithe but doesn't really know why. It was required by his church, so he did it. He has given his money, but he doesn't believe it will work for him or do him any good."

In response to that confession, the Father says, "So be it." God is bound by our words.

That kind of tithing won't work because it is not done in faith. You can have what you say. (Mark 11:23.) That person put his money in and never got anything out of it, because he wasn't careful about what he said.

The Christian who confesses the Word of God over his tithes and offerings experiences results. Since his declaration is based upon Scripture, and the Bible says God will watch over His Word to perform it (Jer. 1:12), God will bring to pass what has been spoken. The Word of God confessed in faith produces great results.

God wants you to watch your mouth and be careful about your confession regarding your tithe. As long as you keep saying it won't work, then it won't. You have to believe it does work. When you present your tithe, say something like this:

"Lord Jesus, take this and worship the Father with it. He's the Most High God, the Possessor of heaven and earth, the Deliverer from all of my enemies. I'm the head and not the tail. I'm above and not beneath. There will be no lack or want in my life.

"So I praise You for meeting my every need. I thank You that the windows of heaven are opened to me and the devourer is rebuked in my behalf. I walk in Your blessings, Lord, for surely they have overtaken me."

After you make a confession like this, Jesus has something to work with. So He goes before the Father and repeats the whole confession you have declared to Him. Then the Father says, "So be it." And heaven has to stand behind your confession of faith.

Jesus makes the same confession in your behalf that you make to Him. Then the Father will bring it about and cause it to come to pass. Tithing isn't a matter of bondage but a matter of order. You have to do it the way God says.

Remember, I started this book by saying God is the Creator and the Owner. That means He is the expert in how everything in this universe functions, including His financial system. You've got to do it the way the expert says it will work. If you get hold of that truth, then any frustrations you may have about giving to God will leave you.

You are giving your money to God's representative here on earth, but you are making a deposit in your heavenly account with your mouth by confessing over your tithe.

Even if the minister who received your tithe doesn't do the right thing with the money, your deposit is still in heaven because you made your confession and worshiped Jesus with it.

I wrote a confession years ago for our tithe that Pat and I use. You'll find it at the end of this book. I encourage you to write your own and then confess it every time you write your tithe check. Don't wait until you get to church to make your confession. Do it at home the moment you set aside your tithe.

THE TITHE AND TITHING WILL PRODUCE PEACE

Years ago, I was studying stewardship. At that time, there was a lot of squabble going on in the world about the Brazilian rain forest. Certain people were talking about how that forest supplied three-fourths of the earth's oxygen and how all those trees were being cut down.

Fear can run rampant through a society as a result of the news media. They tell the bad news, and it spreads like wildfire.

When all that arguing was going on, my mind was racing. I thought, *God, that isn't fair. Some dimwit is cutting down all those trees that produce oxygen for us to breathe around the world. One of these days, they'll cut down so many that we could choke to death! My God, we're helpless. How do we handle this?*

I had that helpless feeling because in the natural I had absolutely no control over this situation. There are times in life

As you mix faith with your tithe and tithing, peace will come into your heart.

when we feel so helpless and power-less. But those are the times when we must remember the Word of God: "Hope thou in God" (Ps. 42:11).

In the midst of the hopelessness, I began to remember the Word of God. I realized that my tithing put me in a position to receive God's blessings in spite of what might be happening around this world. So I said emphatically, "Hey, I've paid my tithes as God directed in His Word, so I'm open to receive from Him. The earth and the fullness thereof belong to Him, so God has control over this situation. I don't care if they cut down all the trees in the world. If God has to evaporate the whole ocean to give me oxygen, I'll have it. I believe in the Most High God, the Possessor of heaven and earth, the Deliverer from all of my enemies. God is in control."

Once I saw that I could put my trust in God, knowing I would have the air to breathe and everything I needed in this life because the whole earth is His, peace came to my heart. I don't care if God has to use the ravens to bring it to me the way He did for Elijah. (1 Kings 17:1-6.) I have faith that it will come to me.

As you mix faith with your tithe and tithing, peace will come into your heart. Every time you present your tithes and make your confession, you are binding it in heaven to work on your behalf.

> *Tithes free me from the fear of lack.*

Words are powerful. God created the world with words. Hebrews 4:12 tells us, "For the word of God is quick, and powerful, and sharper than any twoedged sword, piercing even to the dividing asunder of soul and spirit, and of the joints and marrow, and is a discerner of the thoughts and intents of the heart."

Our words will either snare us or liberate us. (Prov. 6:2.) That is why your confession concerning your tithes is so important. If you trust God, believe Him, and act on His Word, things will change in your life.

Tithe may be an evil word to some people, but it's music to my ears. It's God's plan and His way. It is the first step toward my total deliverance from the instability and corruptibility of the world's financial system. It frees me from the fear of lack.

OPEN AN ACCOUNT IN GOD'S BANKING SYSTEM

I encourage you to become active in His banking system. If you don't tithe, start now. Open a checking account in your name at God's bank. Then you will be able to make deposits into your account as income is received into your life. Giving the tithe is where God's system begins.

Now let's look at how you make deposits in your heavenly savings account.

4

OFFERINGS = SAVINGS ACCOUNT

The second way to put money into God's bank is by making deposits in your heavenly savings account. You make these deposits by giving offerings, which are above your tithes.

There is a difference between paying tithes and giving offerings. Again, the amount of the tithe is 10 percent of your increase. When you give an offering, it is above your tithe. An offering is any amount of money given beyond the 10 percent of your increase.

> *I purpose to plant in every offering because I want to receive on every wave.*

When you give these offerings on earth, you make deposits in your spiritual savings account for future needs.

> When we pay tithes, God promises protection and opened windows of heaven.

In the chapter on tithes, I stated that you couldn't designate your tithe, meaning you couldn't tell the pastor how to spend your tithe. You can designate offerings. You don't have to, but on your offering envelope you can tell the church or ministry how you want the offering spent. For example, you can tell the church that your offering is to go toward missions, a particular missionary, the building fund, or the guest speaker.

I purpose to give every time an offering is received. If I'm in my local church, I'm either paying my tithes or giving an offering. When I'm in other ministry meetings, I give offerings. I purpose to plant in every offering because I want to receive on every wave. If I am consistent with God, then He'll be consistent in His returns to me.

THE PROMISE FOR GIVING OFFERINGS

Each aspect of God's banking system has a promise or reward associated with it. When we pay tithes, God promises protection and opened windows of heaven. Jesus stated the promise of giving in Luke 6:38 when He said, "Give, and it shall be given unto you, good measure, pressed down, shaken together, and running over, shall men give into your bosom. For with the same measure that ye mete withal it shall be measured to you again."

It's important for you to know that God wants to bless you for your giving. The promise of your earthly savings account is the rate of interest that the banks pays you for keeping your account with them. So the "good measure, pressed down, shaken together, and running over, shall men give into your bosom" would be like earning interest in your heavenly savings account. And God doesn't promise to give back exactly what you have given. His rate of return is "running over."

Second Corinthians 9:6-8 tells us some other things about our offerings when we make deposits in our heavenly savings account.

But this I say, He which soweth sparingly shall reap also sparingly; and he which soweth bountifully shall reap also bountifully.

Every man according as he purposeth in his heart, so let him give; not grudgingly, or of necessity: for God loveth a cheerful giver.

And God is able to make all grace abound toward you; that ye, always having all sufficiency in all things may abound to every good work.

2 Corinthians 9:6-8

The apostle Paul wrote about two types of measure here: the measure of the seed and the measure of the heart. Both are important to your giving.

THE MEASURE OF THE SEED

But this I say, He which soweth sparingly shall reap also sparingly; and he which soweth bountifully shall reap also bountifully.

2 Corinthians 9:6

This deals with the natural element of the Law, the measure of the seed. The rule is simple logic: If you plant a small amount of seed, you will reap a small return. If you plant a large amount of seed, you will reap a large return. The more seed you plant, the bigger the harvest you will receive. It all depends on the amount of seed that's sown.

How much you plant and how often you plant play an important part in your return. A farmer doesn't plant a crop once in his lifetime and expect to get a harvest every year. He plants every year so that he has a harvest every year.

Years ago when I first began to understand God's banking system, He dealt with me about consistency, giving every time I was in a service. So I started giving a dollar in every offering. Then one service as I started to pull the dollar bill from my wallet, God asked me, *What are you doing?*

I said, "I'm giving consistently like you taught me."

He replied, *You tightwad. You could give that twenty just as easily as you could that dollar. In fact, if you'll learn to give the biggest bill you can, it will bring you greater freedom.*

Every time I am in a service, I purpose to plant my best seed in every offering because I want the best continuous return. Ecclesiastes 11:1 says, "Cast thy bread upon the waters: for thou shalt find it after many days." I have faith and a confident expectation that my harvest will come back to me on every wave because I keep casting on every wave.

Some people go for long periods of time without giving, and then wonder why they experience barren spells in their lives. If they would consistently give to God, they wouldn't have barren spells. If you want the Lord to be consistent with you, then be consistent with Him. And if you want the best return, give Him your best seed.

THE MEASURE OF THE HEART

Paul dealt with the measure of the heart and the attitude of the giver in verse 7: "Every man according as he purposeth in his heart, so let him give...."

When you give your offering, or make your deposit into your heavenly savings account, you should purpose in your heart. In fact, you should have a twofold purpose:

1. Whatever you are giving will meet the need that you are giving toward.

2. The seed you are planting will be a seed of faith for you to believe God to meet a specific need in your own life.

If the Spirit of God deals with my heart to give a particular offering, He will say something like, "I want you to give that person a hundred dollars to help meet that need."

In obedience, I will plant my seed there, believing that it will be multiplied to him, that he will have the sufficiency to accomplish his purpose. But then I also release my faith for something I'm believing God for in my own life.

Let's say I need money to make some payment that's due. I say, "Father, I am planting seed here so that this need will be met, but also I'm believing You to give back to me so that I can make the payment I owe." You can see the twofold purpose in giving from the heart.

Look again at the first portion of 2 Corinthians 9:7. "Every man according as he purposeth in his heart, so let him give...."

A person should give *according as he purposeth in his heart,* not according to what the preacher purposes. Mark 12:41-44 tells how Jesus watched rich people cast money into the treasury. When He saw a poor widow give two mites, He told the disciples that what she did was great. He wasn't talking about the measure of her seed, because a mite was the smallest amount. He was talking about the measure of her heart. The amount she gave was all she had. The wealthy would not suffer any lack or discomfort because they gave out of their abundance. They had plenty left over, but the widow's gift took the food right out of her mouth. This widow woman wasn't being stingy and withholding from God when she had something to give, nor was she concerned about her own welfare. She could have kept one of the coins, but instead she gave both. She loved God and the temple of God, and she purposed to give God all she had. She was seeking first the kingdom of God and expecting God to take care of all the other things, such as food, clothing, and shelter. The measure of her heart was great.

The measure of the seed is one measure; the measure of the heart is another measure. What makes it so good is when both the measure of the heart and the measure of the seed are big.

Sometimes you are limited in the amount of seed you can plant. You can't give away something you don't have to give. The seed you plant is still great when the measure of your heart is great. By giving your all, you open the bowels of compassion and giving from your heart.

WATCH YOUR PURPOSE WHEN YOU GIVE

Let me tell you a story that demonstrates the importance of purposing in your heart when you give. Entrusted with a publishing company, I am privileged to publish for many wonderful men and women of God. We do our best working with our authors. At one time, I had an author who was never satisfied with the financial arrangements we made with him. He always wanted a better deal, and he would harass and badger me about it. He constantly called me on the phone about it.

It reached the point that I wanted to avoid the man. I began to resent him because he would always throw in this one line when asking for a better deal: "Remember, I'm a brother." He used the fact that he's my brother in the Lord to get into my wallet.

It got so bad that one day I finally looked at him and said, "Tell you what I'm going to do. I'm going to plant seed in your ministry and give you what you want." And I did.

The day came that I needed the return on my investment, and I didn't see it coming. I was thinking, *Now, I've given a lot to this individual. I'm expecting a return, and it's not there.*

I was frustrated, so I went to God in prayer. I said, "Lord, it's not the matter that I haven't planted seed. I've planted lots of seed, particularly in this man's ministry. In fact, Lord, we've become quite close. His hand has been in my back pocket regularly. Now I want my return. I need my return."

The Spirit of God said something that shocked me. He said, *Son, you don't know the difference between giving and giving in.*

When I asked the Lord to explain, He replied, *The governing factor of that law is as every man "purposeth in his heart." What did you purpose in your heart when you gave to that man's ministry?*

It hit me like a ton of bricks. I had purposed to shut him up and get him off my back. I had my return. I received what I had believed for.

Again, 2 Corinthians 9:7 says, "Every man according as he purposeth in his heart, so let him give...." If you purpose to be a blessing, to give cheerfully and correctly, then you get the right return. I hadn't purposed to bless this man. I had purposed to shut him up. Now I was

> *Make sure your motives are right when you give, so you'll get the return you're believing for.*

out of money. It was an expensive lesson to learn, costing thousands of dollars. Now I'm very careful about what I purpose when I give.

Make sure your motives are right when you give, so you'll get the return you're believing for.

No matter whether you're presenting your tithes unto the Lord, giving offerings, or giving alms, you must do it with the right attitude. Although I've already discussed this in the chapter on tithing, I want to remind you about the importance of your attitude.

Let's look at 2 Corinthians 9:7 again. "Every man according as he purposeth in his heart, so let him give; not grudgingly, or of necessity: for God loveth a cheerful giver."

When you give, or make deposits in your heavenly savings account, you must do it cheerfully. Remember what the Greek word for cheerful is? *Hilaros,*[1] from which we get our English word *hilarious.*[2] So you should enjoy giving, and you should do it promptly and willingly and without any hesitation. Offering time isn't designed to be a time of moaning, groaning, and regrets. It should be as joyous and exciting as any other part of the worship service.

You may be doing the right thing, but if it's with the wrong attitude, you will still be wrong. We're giving to God; therefore, we should give with a right attitude. God wants you to give your money with a smile on your face and joy in your heart.

You can undo yourself from the benefits when it comes time to give in the offering if you do it grudgingly or out of necessity. You can't put in your money and sadly think, *There, take it.* Your attitude is wrong. God wants you to give because He is dear to your heart and has supplied you with seed to sow. He wants your heart to be right.

Be Willing and Obedient

When Pat and I first went to work for Kenneth Hagin Ministries, we didn't have much money. I was general manager and traveled with Brother Hagin, while Pat ran the office.

I had two suits, one blue and one brown. Since I was on the road so much, it got old wearing the same two suits all the time, and the suits were wearing out. I wanted a gold sports coat because I could wear any color of slacks with it and have a different look. So I believed God for $75 to buy the gold coat. Nearly 30 years ago, $75 was a lot of money for a sports coat, particularly when you didn't have $75. It was a major step of faith for me to believe that money in.

I'll never forget the day I walked out of the store with that coat in hand. I felt like the NBC peacock. I was proud and just so thankful to my heavenly Father for giving me the money to get the coat.

When the next meeting came around, I put on my new jacket and went into the auditorium to check on things. A minister friend of mine walked into the auditorium. He was just getting started then in the ministry, as I was, and he didn't have much money at that time either. He recognized that I had a new jacket and said to me, "Man, Buddy, that's beautiful. Looks sharp, and fits you good."

I whipped it off and put it on him. The coat looked great on him and fit him perfectly. Just as he was about to take it off, the Spirit of the Lord said, *Give him the coat.* I had believed God for weeks, had worn it only five minutes, and God said to give it away. I wanted to say, "Get behind me, devil." But I knew the voice of God.

> *Your wrong attitude will disqualify you from receiving the return because you aren't doing it the right way.*

I told this young man of God, "Keep the coat on." He said, "Buddy, I didn't mean anything. I wasn't hinting you should give me the coat." I replied, "I know that. The Lord told me to give it to you." That's when I found out that he didn't even own a suit. All he had was a black jacket, and I had two suits, even if they were old.

I went back up to my room and got out my old suit, and began to feel sorry for myself. I almost broke my arm trying to pat myself on the back to comfort myself. But I realized what I was doing, and I said to the Lord, "All right, Lord, I've obeyed You." Immediately, the Lord said, *The willing and the obedient eat the good of the land. Not just the obedient — the willing and obedient.* (Isa. 1:19.) So I got willing right away and rejoiced.

About six weeks later, I was given ten new complete outfits! That's more than I had ever had before. Would I have received those new outfits if I had given grudgingly? I don't think so.

Your wrong attitude will disqualify you from receiving the return because you aren't doing it the right way. When you make deposits into your heavenly account, do it with a right attitude.

Whenever you give to meet the needs of a church, a ministry, or a missionary, you give for the sake of the gospel. It is for the purpose that the gospel might be preached throughout the world. You can expect a return when you do it God's way.

THE HUNDREDFOLD RETURN

There is a distinct law that has to do with giving to the gospel. Jesus talked about this in Mark 10.

> *You can expect a return when you do it God's way.*

And Jesus answered and said, Verily I say unto you, There is no man that hath left house, or brethren, or sisters, or father, or mother, or wife, or children, or lands, for my sake, and the gospel's,

But he shall receive an hundredfold now in this time, houses, and brethren, and sisters, and mothers, and children, and lands, with persecutions; and in the world to come eternal life.

Mark 10:29,30

From what Jesus said here, we know that disciples, followers of Jesus, have the right to expect a return. In the time the Gospels were written, Christians experienced much persecution, imprisonment, torture, and even death. Often, becoming a Christian meant the loss of one's natural family rights, which would have included a share in the family wealth. In some countries around the world this is still true today. Jesus' precious promise is that we have a reward in this lifetime, as well as the one to come. Man may deny us, but Jesus won't as long as we follow Him.

I want you to realize that the hundredfold return is about an exceedingly generous return, not necessarily a specific dollar amount. Whenever we give something for the gospel's sake, God restores it to us in a glorious, exceeding, abundant way. You can believe your return is exactly a hundredfold return on what you gave. There is nothing wrong with that. I prefer to believe that God can do exceedingly abundantly. He causes my seed to produce to its fullest extent, and to the best of its capabilities.

The hundredfold return won't really work for you unless you have been tithing. Now, I would imagine every believer has planted seed and given into the gospel at some time but has never gotten a return and wonders why.

Some of God's laws haven't worked because believers haven't understood them and haven't properly applied them. There was a time in my life when I wanted to believe God for the hundredfold return, but I hadn't presented my tithe. Satan stole my offering seed, and I had nothing. That's just the way it works. If you don't ever tithe, you can forget about receiving any return on your offerings.

It's a blessing to receive the hundredfold return on our giving, but there is one part of the equation that many people don't like. You may feel the same way about it. In Mark 10:30, Jesus said, "But he shall receive an hundredfold now in this time, houses, and brethren, and sisters, and mothers, and children, and lands, with persecutions...."

Notice the last phrase in this verse: "with persecutions." That stops many people from receiving God's blessings. They begin to be persecuted for something they received as part of the blessings of God.

> *When you obey God and give offerings, you make deposits in your heavenly savings account with that investment.*

Harsh criticism can hurt. Think about this for a moment. Let's say God has blessed you in some way and, as a result, you are led to go down a certain path in your life. You feel so thankful and rejoice in the favor of God. But then someone becomes jealous about it and lashes out at you with unkind words.

When that persecution comes, you start to back away from the new path you have just taken in your life. You change course and turn from the decision you had made when you received God's favor. In other words, you back away from the Word of God.

When persecutions come, and Jesus said they would, we have to keep our eyes on God and move down the path He has designed for us.

KNOW WHERE TO INVEST

Now, if you don't care what happens in your future, then don't bother to give any offerings, or make deposits in your heavenly savings account. But if you're concerned at all about your future, I suggest that you open an account in heaven and give.

It's important that you pray about where to invest your offerings, so that you can earn a return on your investment. As you pray about it, God will speak to you and tell you where to invest and how much.

When you obey God and give offerings, you make deposits in your heavenly savings account with that investment. This way God insures your future. As you give, you will have the return in the future when some necessity arises. You will have your return when needed because you will have previously given.

Most of the time we wait until we find ourselves in trouble. Then we give in a hurry, thinking our problem will get fixed. That's contrary to the law of giving.

In the natural realm, different seeds have different amounts of growing time. One type of seed may need three months before a harvest is produced. Another seed may produce in one month. It depends upon the seed we are sowing and the ground we are planting in as to how quickly we reap the harvest. The same is true in the spiritual realm.

We need to make good investments. We need to watch where we give our offerings when we make deposits in our heavenly savings account.

Let's look again at Mark 10. Jesus said in verse 29, "...There is no man that hath left house...." Notice that *house* is singular in this verse.

"But then in verse 30 Jesus said, But he shall receive an hundredfold now in this time, houses...." That means the return is plural, or a multiple. We give away one, and we will receive more.

Our return depends on planting or making deposits the way God says. First we have to give. Again, in Luke 6:38 Jesus said, "Give, and it shall be given unto you; good measure, pressed down, and shaken together, and running over, shall men give into your bosom. For with the same measure that ye mete withal it shall be measured to you again."

> *Make sure you plant in good ground.*

There is a law that Jesus was talking about here. We can see this by backing up to verse 37.

Judge not, and ye shall not be judged: condemn not, and ye shall not be condemned: forgive, and ye shall be forgiven:

Give, and it shall be given unto you....

Luke 6:37,38

Jesus told us there is a law in operation. It's the law of action and reaction, or the law of sowing and reaping.

He broke it down on the financial level, so that we can see how it works. If we give, it will be given to us, good measure, pressed down, shaken together, and running over. In the book of Malachi God said that the windows of heaven would be open to us. That's fullness! That's abundance!

If you make natural investments, you watch where you put your money because you want the best return on your money. Therefore, you will be careful about where you put it. You won't invest in something that isn't doing well. You want something that's performing. It doesn't matter how big it is, as long as it's producing.

You should be just as wise to watch where you deposit your money when you invest in the things of God. One kind of ground just doesn't yield as well as another. Make sure you plant in good ground.

Plant wherever God directs you to plant. There will be times when the Spirit of God knows about places that need your investment, and He will direct you at that moment. If you have no specific direction from God about where to plant, then follow your own leading. Watch for the fruit, and if it's acceptable, plant there.

One day the Lord said to me, *Only give to a giver.* I didn't understand why, so I asked Him about it. He responded,

Because if you give to a giver, he (or she) will know how to give to another person. Then that person will give to still another person. That way it keeps multiplying in the kingdom.

God is interested in multiplying your seed. That is why you give offerings to givers. It lines up with the Word of God. Jesus said:

> **For he that hath, to him shall be given: and he that hath not, from him shall be taken even that which he hath.**
>
> **Mark 4:25**

If you give to people who are stingy, then you stop the multiplication factor. Once you stop it, it can't go any further. It can't increase. Think of it like water that doesn't move. It stagnates and becomes unproductive. Scum covers its surface. Another example is that the rich soil of Iowa is more productive and easier to get a crop from than the desert soil of Death Valley. It's important for you to give offerings to someone who will give.

I'm a giver. There are other ministers I know who are also givers. They're good ground. When I give to them, it always pays off. I know it will yield for me. I give to them; then, in turn, they give to others who are givers. Thus, we all receive a return from our giving.

If I don't know whether or not someone is a giver, I'm not apt to give to him or her. If I do give, it's because I consider that person to be poor. Then I give from the standpoint and receive based upon the promise of return when giving to the poor. We will look at the subject of giving alms in the next chapter.

Whenever I give above my tithe, I always decide whether it's an offering or alms. Then I plant accordingly and exercise my faith for the promise that goes with what I am planting. It's important that you understand what you are doing so you can properly exercise your faith and receive the return.

HONOR GOD WITH YOUR GIVING

We honor God with our gifts. We apply Matthew 6:33 and seek first the kingdom of God. We proclaim that which we have and honor God as we do it. We are seeking the plan of God more than we seek our own way.

Our own selfishness would tell us to hang on to money because we will have great need of it. But when we begin to honor God with our offerings, the truth of God's Word comes forth. Proverbs 3:9 says, "Honour the Lord with thy substance...." Substance comes in all forms. For instance, Scripture tells us that faith is substance. (Heb. 11:1.) So you can see how faith is involved when you give.

If I give in every offering, then I am involving my faith as I give. One of two things had to transpire for you to obtain those finances that you are giving: either you worked and earned it, or you believed God for it. Either way, it still belongs to God because the earth and the fullness thereof belong to Him. (Ps. 24:1.) The food that you ate grew out of God's earth, and He gave you the strength to work and earn your money.

Give honor to God every time you present your offering. Remember, you are making a deposit in your heavenly savings account that will earn interest in your behalf. You will receive His blessings because you have given your offerings in His honor.

DON'T PUT CONFIDENCE IN YOUR MONEY

As we stated earlier, there is a reward and promise that go with offerings, but there can be danger, too. The danger is that you will be tempted to trust in yourself and your wealth, rather than in God. As you operate God's system, you will experience financial abundance. The devil will come along and try to get you to trust in your riches, rather than in God. As you prosper, keep your trust in God and His Word.

When you put your money in the earth's system, it is subject to the earth's environment: moths, rust, and thieves. If you plant in your heavenly savings account, your investment is subject to God's environment. What is so important about that?

God's environment is abundance, and it never changes. The world's system is full of rust or decay. The value of a nation's currency fluctuates. One day the dollar is worth so much, and the next week it is worth less. Our treasure doesn't decay in heaven; it is multiplied with interest.

The measure of your seed, the measure of your heart, the frequency with which you give, the ground you're giving into, and your attitude when giving, all affect your return.

Now let's consider the third way of making deposits in our heavenly account, which is giving alms, or giving to the poor.

5

ALMS = GIVING TO
THE POOR = LOANS

The third way to invest money in your heavenly bank account is by giving alms, or giving to the poor. Giving offerings and giving alms are two distinct types of giving, but they both affect your future.

As we have learned, there are certain rules for paying tithes and giving offerings. The same is true with alms.

You must have the right attitude when giving to the poor. You can't be haughty or have a superior attitude. Neither can you be condescending: *Here's a little crumb for you.* To act in either manner would undo the purpose of your giving and nullify your return. Be careful not to get caught up in pride.

The Lord never belittled poor people. On the contrary, He provided for them in the Law, and He would rebuke the Jewish society when it neglected the poor. (Isa. 3:14,15.) In fact, Judaism and Christianity are the only major religions that care for the poor and do something to change their circumstances.

You will find numerous instructions in Exodus, Leviticus, and Deuteronomy concerning the treatment of the poor, widows, orphans, and strangers. A number of Scriptures in Proverbs deal with attitudes concerning the poor.

The Lord is very clear about not being hardhearted or cynical concerning the poor. Neither are we to take advantage of them.

> **If there be among you a poor man of one of thy brethren within any of thy gates in thy land which the Lord thy God giveth thee, thou shalt not harden thine heart, nor shut thine hand from thy poor brother:**
>
> **But thou shalt open thine hand wide unto him, and shalt surely lend him sufficient for his need, in that which he wanteth.**
>
> **Beware that there be not a thought in thy wicked heart, saying, The seventh year, the year of release, is at hand; and thine eye be evil against thy poor brother, and thou givest him nought; and he cry unto the Lord against thee, and it be sin unto thee.**
>
> **Thou shalt surely give him, and thine heart shall not be grieved when thou givest unto him: because that for this thing**

the Lord thy God shall bless thee in all thy works, and in all that thou puttest thine hand unto.

For the poor shall never cease out of the land: therefore I command thee, saying, Thou shalt open thine hand wide unto thy brother, to thy poor, and to thy needy, in thy land.

Deuteronomy 15:7-11

This doesn't mean that we give indiscriminately, for con artists — people who play upon your emotions and make you think they're poor so you'll give to them — exist.

Notice that the Scripture says "brethren." That's talking about people you know, people in your church, and family members. It doesn't mean you should not give to the beggar or homeless person on the street. There are Scriptures that address giving to strangers. You give when and where God tells you to give. You just need to be led by the Spirit in your giving.

We should lend to our brother that which he has need of. This doesn't necessarily mean a person who is totally poor, although that can apply. It's talking about a brother or sister in the Lord, in the family of faith, being in need or in want at that particular time. It doesn't mean that his whole life is in devastation. It just means he's in need or want at that moment.

If you hear that your brother or sister in the Lord has a need, and you have it to give, you should fulfill that need. We are not to ignore the poor and withhold our help. Proverbs 3:27 says,

"Withhold not good from them to whom it is due, when it is in the power of thine hand to do it." You can see that the Lord cares for all people and has made provision for those who suffer lack.

Some people (the same ones who don't want to tithe) might say, "Well, giving to the poor is Old Testament law, and I am free from the law." Let me show you an example of New Testament alms giving.

In 2 Corinthians 8, the apostle Paul was talking about money, poverty, and gifts for the church. Let me give you a little background.

There was a severe famine in Judea, and the church in Jerusalem was suffering. So Paul was receiving offerings from the churches he had founded to help their brethren in Jerusalem. (1 Cor. 16:1-4.) In writing to the Corinthians (in the region of Achaia, the southern part of Greece), he bragged on the generosity of the Macedonians (brethren in the northern part of Greece).

The Macedonian Christians had suffered much persecution. Though they were not rich, they were liberal and cheerful givers. They didn't withhold anything when it was in their power to give. (Prov. 3:27.) In verse 2 of 2 Corinthians 8, Paul wrote:

> **How that in a great trial of affliction the abundance of their joy and their deep poverty abounded unto the riches of their liberality.**

Then verse 4 of the same chapter says:

Praying us with much intreaty that we would receive the gift, and take upon us the fellowship of the ministering to the saints.

There is a point here about ministering to the saints. Another Scripture declares that we are to be kind, especially unto those of the household of faith, those who are walking in like fashion as we. (Gal. 6:10.)

There should be expressions of love to our brothers and sisters in the Lord. In other words, we should be taking care of our own. Just as we have a responsibility to take care of our parents, children, and grandchildren, we have the same responsibility to take care of those who believe as we do.

Paul was talking about our abounding in something. Second Corinthians 8:7 says:

Therefore, as ye abound in every thing, in faith, and utterance, and knowledge, and in all diligence, and in your love to us, see that ye abound in this grace also.

What grace is he referring to here? He is referring to giving. "Giving" in this verse refers to giving to the needy. Therefore, giving alms is just as much New Testament as it is Old Testament.

Because Jesus said, "For ye have the poor always with you" (Matt. 26:11), some people have thought that they aren't required to do anything about the poor. But that wasn't Jesus' point. Jesus was stating a present reality: There will always be poor people in this earth as long as the devil is the ruler of the earth. That doesn't mean that Christians can ignore the poor.

Let's look at that Scripture in its context.

Now when Jesus was in Bethany, in the house of Simon the leper,

There came unto him a woman having an alabaster box of very precious ointment, and poured it on his head, as he sat at meat.

But when his disciples saw it, they had indignation, saying, To what purpose is this waste?

For this ointment might have been sold for much, and given to the poor.

When Jesus understood it, he said unto them, Why trouble ye the woman? for she hath wrought a good work upon me.

For ye have the poor always with you; but me ye have not always.

For in that she hath poured this ointment on my body, she did it for my burial.

Matthew 26:6-12

The disciples called this woman's gift a waste because they didn't understand the purpose and significance of her actions. Part of their problem was lack of understanding. The other part of their problem was timing. The disciples were not wrong in being concerned about the poor. It's just that their timing was wrong. They would always have an opportunity to minister to the poor, but they wouldn't always have an opportunity to minister physically to Jesus.

Jesus was preparing for His death, burial, and resurrection, so He interpreted the woman's gift as preparation for burial. He was seeing into the future, something the disciples couldn't do. Jesus wanted them to understand that right timing is just as important as right action. Right timing plus right action plus right motive produces righteousness.

I want to point out one other thing about Matthew 26:11. Scholars believe that when Jesus said, "For ye have the poor always with you," He was quoting from Deuteronomy 15:11. If Jesus was quoting from Deuteronomy 15, then He knew that the Father wanted His people to open their hands — and not just a little bit but WIDE — to their brothers. Therefore, Jesus wasn't telling the disciples not to give; He was instructing them in their timing of giving to the poor.

HOW DO PEOPLE BECOME POOR?

Poverty does not come from the Lord. He doesn't have it to give. We've already seen that in the first chapter. Someone who owns all the world and the fullness thereof is not poor. Heaven is not a poor place. Its streets are paved with gold, and its gates are made from precious stones.

In John 10:10 Jesus said, "The thief cometh not, but for to steal, and to kill, and to destroy: I am come that they might have life, and that they might have it more abundantly." That means life in its fullest sense. Jesus changes the lives of people for the better.

It could be that Satan has stolen from the poor. It could be that a curse passed from generation to generation is operating in their lives, and that poverty has been in the family for several generations. Possibly, they have not learned how to manage money and make wise financial decisions.

Often people have made themselves poor and have created lack in their lives simply because they don't act on the Word of God.

Now, this "poorness" may have been manifested in the physical realm, such as in finances or goods, but lack begins when people fail to receive God's Word. Consequently, they make themselves poor.

The good news is that no one has to stay poor. God has an abundant life for whosoever will! Jesus defeated the devil, gave us back our dominion, and made us heirs of God. If we'll obey the Word of God and the Spirit of God, we won't stay poor.

We're talking about God's plan for producing wealth in your life. Giving your tithes is where you begin. Then you give offerings, and you give to the poor. You must do all three to experience supernatural abundance.

LENDING TO THE LORD

Just as with paying tithes and giving offerings, there is a promise of God's blessings with alms. Proverbs 19:17 tells us the promise that accompanies giving to the poor.

> **He that hath pity upon the poor lendeth unto the Lord; and that which he hath given will he pay him again.** [God will repay the loan.]
>
> **Proverbs 19:17**

Giving alms is the same as lending to the Lord. And God's promise for lending is that He will repay.

One of God's names is El Shaddai.[1] He is not El Cheapo! El Shaddai means that God is the exceeding, abundant, and lavish gift-giving God. He told Abraham that He, the I Am, was Abraham's exceeding, great reward. (Gen. 15:1.)

> *El Shaddai means that God is the exceeding, abundant, and lavish gift-giving God.*

Our God isn't cheap or stingy. He doesn't pay back in a cheap fashion. He gives a full-fledged blessing. So when God repays, He pays back with a better rate of interest than you can get anywhere on this earth!

The practice of giving to the poor is proper and right, but you must keep it in the right perspective, or it will get out of proportion and you could miss God's best in what He wants you to do regarding alms.

Again, Proverbs 19:17 says, "He that hath pity upon the poor lendeth unto the Lord...." As I studied the Hebrew words in this verse, I found some interesting meanings of these words. Let's consider some of them.

While examining the Hebrew word translated pity, I found this meaning: "to bend or to stoop in kindness to an inferior; to favor."[2] Let me give you a picture of how this can be.

When I was on a mission trip to Mexico, we saw beggars sitting on the sidewalks of its cities with their hands held out to receive. Our love and compassion made us want to reach out to help them. But for us to give to them in an act of kindness meant we had to bend over or stoop down. In other words, we were showing favor to those needy ones. We had blessings they didn't have, and we were extending our hands of blessing down to them.

So "he that hath pity on the poor" means someone is showing favor and is bending over in kindness toward those in need.

According to 1 Corinthians 12:27, you are the body of Christ and a member in particular. When you reach out to others, it's the same as Jesus reaching out. He is the Head; you are the Body.

Look at Proverbs 3:27 from *The Message Bible:*

> **Never walk away from someone who deserves help; your hand is God's hand for that person.**

You are God's hand extended to others. As a partaker of His favor and grace, you have the inheritance; therefore, you reach out to those in need and share your blessings.

There are more ways to bend over than just in the physical sense. Many times it's more than money that's involved. God is concerned about our spirit, soul, and body. Giving alms is a physical demonstration; yet there is both spiritual application and soulish application that will be profitable to us.

When I studied the word *poor* in Proverbs 19:17, I found that it means "dangling, weak or thin; lean, needy."[3] That word is speaking of the physical aspect of someone who is weak, thin, lean, and needy.

As I studied further, I found that there are four Hebrew words translated *poor.* When using the word *poor,* it depends on what area you are dealing with as to how you will establish its meaning. There is more involved than the simple matter of someone without money.

> **For the oppression of the poor, for the sighing of the needy, now will I arise, saith the Lord; I will set him in safety from him that puffeth at him.**
>
> **Psalm 12:5**

Notice the phrase "for the oppression of the poor." This *poor* means "depressed in mind or circumstances."[4] When oppression comes against your mind, your mind is poor at that moment. It has lack. It has need of something.

When speaking do you mean spiritually poor, mentally poor, or physically poor? No matter what realm you are referring to, you still are in lack and need.

Another word for poor means "make self poor."[5] People can make themselves poor. They can put themselves in lack or want. They can be self-deceived. James 1:22 says that if you aren't a doer of the Word, you deceive yourself. If you don't do the Word, you lack the Word, which makes you poor and needy.

As you can see, someone who is poor can be poor in spirit, soul, or body. Thank God that He is interested in all three.

Now let's go back to our text from Proverbs 19:17. Again, it says, "He that hath pity upon the poor lendeth unto the Lord."

He that hath pity is the one who bends or stoops in kindness to show favor to the poor. In some way this person gives help or shows kindness to the poor one. It could be money, a meal, clothes, or a job. The poor is the one who is in lack, need, or want. Though the giver gives to the poor person, he is actually lending to the Lord, making a loan to the Lord.

I was surprised when I saw the meaning of the word *lend* as used in this verse. When thinking in terms of lending, I thought basically of giving. That's just how my mind clicked on that word. I was giving to the Lord; therefore, I would get a return on my investment.

But the word *lend* here means "to twine, to unite."[6] He who gives to the poor entwines or unites with the Lord. Meditate on that for a while, and you'll begin to see how powerful that statement is. You can't get hooked up to the Lord any better way than that!

God is a spirit. When we give to the poor, we are entwining and uniting them with the Lord.

And when we give to the poor, we have this promise:

...and that which he has given He will repay to him.

Proverbs 19:17 AMP

123

God pays good interest, more than any bank is paying here on earth!

DON'T EXPECT PAYMENT FROM PEOPLE

When we lend to people, most of the time we want it paid back. The Bible way is to lend and not expect it back from man. That will be hard on some people. They might say, "Well, I didn't have it to lend." Then they shouldn't have lent it to begin with.

Proverbs 19:17 says that God repays the one who gives to the poor.

In Luke 6, Jesus affirmed it.

And if ye lend to them of whom ye hope to receive, what thank have ye? for sinners also lend to sinners, to receive as much again.

But love ye your enemies, and do good, and lend, hoping for nothing again; and your reward shall be great, and ye shall be the children of the Highest: for he is kind unto the unthankful and to the evil.

Be ye therefore merciful, as your Father also is merciful.

Luke 6:34-36

Often when we see a need, we tend to look within ourselves and think, *No, I need that,* or, *But if I lend it, I won't get it back.* According to the scriptural pattern, when we lend we should not expect it back. Instead we should expect the Lord to return to us. Look to God as the supplier of your need instead of looking to man.

Remember, God is the One who will reward you, and the One who will pay you back. Look in the right place, at the right source. If you have your eyes in the wrong direction, you will become frustrated and negate what God is doing on your behalf.

When you give to the poor, you are lending to the Lord. In other words, you have put yourself in a position to be blessed by God. And you are to do it with a certain purpose and attitude of the heart.

On a mission trip to Mexico, I began to question myself about giving to beggars on the street. I wondered, *Why am I giving? Is it to salve my conscience at that moment, or is it because I've purposed in my heart to give out of love?* I began to examine the intent of my heart.

Again, 2 Corinthians 9:7 says, "Every man according as he purposeth in his heart, so let him give...." You can expressly show favor and unite people with God by sharing with them. But there's a Bible way to do it. Just because you give to someone doesn't necessarily mean you have done it right. You have to understand what you are doing with regard to your purpose of heart.

People can become caught up in something. Take telethons, for example. Some people become involved out of inspiration at the moment. Others participate out of guilt. They haven't done what they feel they should have done, so they want to salve their conscience.

Whatever situation you may face, you must be willing to lend without expecting a return from the one you gave to.

There is a law involved in lending to the poor: God repays. You can be sure that the return will come, but don't make the mistake of expecting it from the wrong place.

Let's say you are giving to the poor through some charitable organization. You have purposed in your heart to give in that way, so you expect a return. Now you have planted seed in that organization, but you aren't looking for them to give you anything. Yet there is still a reward due to you because of your giving. You obeyed the Word of God and gave to the poor, and God will give back to you. He said He would do it in response to your giving. That's the law.

By giving food, clothes, money, and other basic things to the poor, I am assured that I will have those basics in my life. Doesn't every seed reproduce after its own kind? Then I'm taking care that my life will be like Jesus describes in Matthew 6:31 when He says, "Therefore take no thought, saying, What shall we eat? or, What shall we drink? or, Wherewithal shall we be clothed?"

Giving to the poor brings an equality that no government program will ever be able to do. Because we are bestowing the grace and favor of God upon others, something governments can't do, we pull people up to our level and cause them to be seated with us.

When you're making deposits in your heavenly account by giving to the poor, make sure you do so with the right motives, the right timing, and the right actions.

6

MAKING DEPOSITS IN YOUR HEAVENLY ACCOUNT

As was pointed out in previous chapters, God has a heavenly banking system with a purpose and plan for its monetary structure. It's important that you realize a heavenly account has been set up in your name. You utilize God's financial system by making spiritual deposits in your heavenly account.

Spiritual deposits are made when you invest your money into the work of God here on earth as you pay your tithes, give offerings, and give alms. Though you give these financial gifts to human beings here on earth, God receives your gifts and deposits them into your heavenly account. Your deposits then will earn interest in your behalf if you have done it with the right attitude, motive, and perspective.

Your understanding of the principles that govern your heavenly account are as important as of those involved in your earthly bank account. The two work in harmony. There are rules and regulations with each type of giving, whether it's tithes (checking), offerings (savings), or alms (loans).

When you make a deposit at your bank, you had better do it according to the guidelines that have been set up by that institution. The simple rule is that you must put something in before you can take something out.

If you go to a bank, you can't develop your own system as to how you will deposit and withdraw your money. You must follow the rules designed by that bank.

It's the same way with God's banking system. You have to do it His way. It isn't a matter of legalism or bondage. God simply has a system. If you operate it His way, it will work. Most people don't even know God has a financial system, much less rules they have to follow.

Most Christians want to make withdrawals from their heavenly account, believing that God meets their needs, when they have never made a deposit. This is where the mistake is made. They say, "I need an answer from God," but they have made no investment in the kingdom of God. When they face tough situations in life and need answers to their questions, they have nothing to draw from. We have to put something in before we can take anything out.

You open your account in heaven by making an initial deposit. You have to continue to make deposits, so that your account can build up. Then you begin to earn interest.

Your paycheck on earth represents a portion of your life. It's money you earned with your labor, and in some cases with your sweat. You have to take it to the bank and deposit it into your account, so that you will be able to make withdrawals as needs arise in your life.

The same is true with your heavenly account. As I said earlier, the two work in harmony. When you make deposits here on earth by paying tithes, giving offerings, and giving alms, you are simultaneously making spiritual deposits in your heavenly account. It is an investment in your spiritual life. And as a result, you can call on God's Word, believing that your needs will be met in your life here on earth.

God will compound the interest you receive on your investment by multiplying the seed that's sown. That's His plan. The world has tried to copy God's system to a degree. There are limitations as to how far it can go. But God, who has all the ability, can bring a return on your investment and make it work on your behalf.

TREASURES IN HEAVEN

Lay not up for yourselves treasures upon earth, where moth and rust doth corrupt, and where thieves break through and steal:

But lay up for yourselves treasures in heaven, where neither moth nor rust doth corrupt, and where thieves do not break through nor steal:

For where your treasure is, there will your heart be also.

Matthew 6:19-21

Notice again in verse 19 that Jesus said, "Lay not up for yourselves treasures upon earth...." Too many Christians are doing exactly what Jesus said not to do. They are laying up treasures here on earth. God wants them to prosper, to have the best, but they have only made their investments here on earth. They have put it all in the one spot, and it hasn't paid off for them.

Instead of investing only in your natural account here on earth, put some money in your heavenly account, too. You won't be making a spiritual investment that earns interest until you do.

There's nothing wrong with a natural account. I believe we should have natural accounts, and Pat and I do, but you can't put your confidence in natural accounts. If you expect to prosper through your investments in the natural realm alone, you will miss out on the blessings from God.

As Jesus said, when you lay up treasures upon earth, then moth and rust will corrupt, and thieves will break through and steal. Satan is the god of this world. (2 Cor. 4:4.) When you put your confidence in things here on the earth, you place yourself in his path. Then he has authority to take from you what he wills. That's what has happened to us many times. Like a worm, Satan will eat up everything he can.

To rust simply means to decay. As I mentioned earlier, the value of a dollar fluctuates. Some years its value goes down, or decays. But when you invest your money in heaven, its value increases.

In Matthew 6:20 Jesus says, "But lay up for yourselves treasures in heaven...." You are doing this for yourself, not for God. God doesn't need your dollars with Him in heaven to accomplish what He wants. The deposits you are making in your heavenly account are for your benefit here on earth.

God has you make your deposits in heaven so that they will be protected. The worm can't eat it. It won't decay. It won't rust out from under you. No thief can steal it from heaven because the only thief that ever existed in heaven, Lucifer, was kicked out. When you make these deposits in heaven, you can know that God's blessings will be there for you.

> **Charge them that are rich in this world, that they be not highminded, nor trust in uncertain riches, but in the living God, who giveth us richly all things to enjoy;**
>
> **That they do good, that they be rich in good works, ready to distribute, willing to communicate;**
>
> **Laying up in store for themselves a good foundation against the time to come, that they may lay hold on eternal life.**
>
> 1 Timothy 6:17-19

The word *communicate* in verse 18 means to give. In that day, giving was different from the way it is today. Back then, people didn't have bank accounts like we do now. When they would "lay up in store," it meant that they put it in a place where it was safe, protected, and taken care of. The elements couldn't get to it.

We aren't laying up our money in store for God. He doesn't need it. We are laying it up in store for ourselves.

Continuing on in verse 19, it says, "Laying up in store for themselves a good foundation against the time to come, that they may lay hold on eternal life." Someone might say, "You see, we're supposed to lay it up for when we get over into eternal life." We have eternal life now!

We don't have to wait until we get to heaven. We can have it now. Jesus said we have life and have it more abundantly. (John 10:10.) We aren't talking about laying up our investment for over there. God has no need for it. He has plenty; in fact, He will give us some of His. You need to realize that it's being laid up in store for you now. *Now* is present tense.

Notice these words in 1 Timothy 6:19: "Laying up in store for themselves a good foundation against the time to come." When is "the time to come"? When we need it. We are living in the now. The time to come is now.

WHEN "THINGS" HAVE PEOPLE

God doesn't mind people having things. He just doesn't want things having people. It all has to do with attitude. You have to trust in the living God, not in things.

I have seen people who had enough money to buy anything they wanted. Some of them were multimillionaires. Yet their money couldn't purchase for them what they really needed.

People like that are looking to things as their source. They may think they will be financially successful simply because they have a really sharp mind; but as long as their confidence and trust are in their abilities and their riches, somewhere along the way they will fail. It doesn't make any difference how much money someone has. Money can't buy life.

If your trust and confidence are in God and you have made deposits, not just in your earthly account but in your heavenly account, you are on good ground for God's blessings to overtake you.

You've probably heard people mention their little nest egg. The whole idea is for them to have something put aside for a rainy day. Their rainy day comes. They can count on it. They have laid up for that exact purpose.

If you lay up treasure in heaven, it will be there for your pleasure. It is not out of fear or frustration. The treasure is there for a purpose.

There is a danger when you put your trust in money. Your trust needs to be in God, not in those things or dollars. When you make deposits in your heavenly account, you place your trust in God. He is the One you count on to pay off for you.

In the natural realm, if you put your trust in a bank and sock away your money out of fear for that rainy day, that day will come. Your money will be uncertain because everything in the natural is uncertain. It's always changing.

God doesn't change. When He gives His Word, He watches over it to perform it. (Jer. 1:12 AMP.) You can count on your return when you have need of it. That's where your confidence has to be.

First Timothy 6:10 says, "For the love of money is the root of all evil...." I remind you that money is not evil. It's the love of money that is evil. It's what you do with money and your attitude toward it that allow evil or good to come forth.

As long as you have love, confidence, and trust in God, you will have plenty of money. It's a matter of where your confidence lies. Some people do not realize that money can deceive them.

In Mark 4, Jesus shared the parable of the sower and the seed. He explains how the seed is placed in different ground.

And these are they which are sown among thorns; such as hear the word,

And the cares of this world, and the deceitfulness of riches, and the lusts of other things entering in, choke the word, and it becometh unfruitful.

Mark 4:18,19

Wrong thinking and wrong attitudes divert their focus.

The problem is a wrong attitude. A wrong attitude about money causes problems. Again, money isn't evil. But if you love that money and trust in it, you're standing on the wrong ground. Keep your love and trust in God; then you will have plenty of money to spend here on earth.

Many people make the mistake of putting their confidence in money. They become deceived, and they keep their eyes on their money rather than on God.

Wrong thinking and wrong attitudes divert their focus. Thus, the Word of God is choked and becomes unproductive in their lives. (Mark 4:19.) When the Word is choked, their faith doesn't work and they are unable to hear the Holy Spirit leading them.

We are His stewards of what He has given us here on earth, while He is the Steward of what we have deposited in our heavenly account. Glory to God!

LET GOD BE YOUR MONEY MANAGER

When you deposit money in your bank account here on earth, that money belongs to you. You just allow someone else to manage your money for you. You can draw it out of your account at any time because the money still belongs to you.

We are in covenant with God. We manage all God has entrusted us with here on earth, so He can draw from it any time He wants. The same is true in heaven. When we invest in our heavenly bank account, we put our treasures in heaven. God manages our money, and He knows how to do it.

The exciting thing is that we are partners with God. We are His stewards of what He has given us here on earth, while He is the Steward of what we have deposited in our heavenly account. Glory to God!

Although we are giving to man, our gifts are deposited in our heavenly account. Therefore, we have to say something about it. We make a confession about our tithes, about our offerings, and about our giving to the poor.

Remember, as has been pointed out in earlier chapters, the apostle Paul wrote, "Every man according as he pur-poseth in his heart, so let him give…" (2 Cor. 9:7). Vocalize what you purpose in your heart. Speaking is a vital part of your deposit into your heavenly account.

On earth, the natural realm, we make deposits through man. In heaven, the spiritual realm, it is through confession. When you tithe and give, you are to make your confession to God. Let's now look at how we make withdrawals from the heavenly account.

7

MAKING WITHDRAWALS FROM
YOUR HEAVENLY ACCOUNT

In previous chapters we learned about making deposits in our heavenly account. Now let's discover how to make withdrawals from this account.

When you put your money in a bank here on earth, at some point you have to withdraw it. The same is true with your heavenly account. Once deposits have been made in heaven, you can make withdrawals.

You make withdrawals the same way you make deposits: with your confession.

FIVE REQUIREMENTS TO WITHDRAW

1. Decide.

To make withdrawals from heaven's banking account, the first step is to make a decision. In the natural, when you go to the bank to withdraw money from your account, you must decide how much you want and for what reason.

The Bible says we have not because we ask not, and we ask and receive not because we ask amiss. (James 4:2,3.) If you don't have the money to do what you want to do, it's because you haven't asked God, or because you have asked apart from the Word of God.

> *Withdrawing your treasure from heaven starts with a decision process.*

Often we haven't made a proper decision. Our decisions must be quality decisions. My book *7 Steps to a Quality Decision* explores how to make quality decisions.

Our tithes and offerings are ways we plant seed into the kingdom of God, or make investments in our heavenly account. Many times we have treated our giving so loosely and casually that it has had no meaning to us. That's a big mistake. It is necessary to be very exact, very precise, about our giving.

I have found that certain keys protect me when I make deposits in my heavenly bank account. When my increase comes, I write my tithe check. I don't mix tithes and offerings. They are two different banking operations with two different sets of promises. I always write my tithe and offering checks separately.

You might say, "Well, I need to save money and not have so many different checks." But if it confuses your faith, I would think you would want to make the separation.

I write my tithe check as soon as I get my increase. I don't wait to write it when I reach the church. I'm putting God first. I give to God immediately before any of that money is spent on other things.

If you don't have a bank account and prefer to use cash, I recommend that you separate your tithe as soon as you get your check cashed. You should put your money in an envelope and take it with you to the next church service you attend.

Withdrawing your treasure from heaven starts with a decision process. Begin by asking, "What is it that I'm believing God for?" You must do that in order to focus your faith and zero in on exactly what you want from God. Set your priorities.

Before you go to the grocery store, you say, "We need eggs, milk, bread." You make a decision and then go after whatever it is you need. The same is true when you go before God. As you learn to walk in this process and function according to His plan, His will, and His Word, God will bless you.

So, first, make your decision.

2. Withdraw From Heaven by Faith and Actions.

The second step is to lay hold on it in faith.

> **And Jesus answering saith unto them, Have faith in God.**
>
> **For verily I say unto you, That whosoever shall say unto this mountain, Be thou removed, and be thou cast into the sea; and shall not doubt in his heart, but shall believe that those things which he saith shall come to pass; he shall have whatsoever he saith.**
>
> **Therefore I say unto you, What things soever ye desire, when ye pray, believe that ye receive them, and ye shall have them.**
>
> **Mark 11:22-24**

When putting money in your heavenly account, you give to men here on earth, but God receives it in heaven.

> **Give, and it shall be given unto you; good measure, pressed down, and shaken together, and running over, shall men give into your bosom. For with the same measure that ye mete withal it shall be measured to you again.**
>
> **Luke 6:38**

Jesus said that it's men who will give into your bosom. Man is the vehicle through which God's blessing will come to you in return.

Unfortunately, some people are still expecting God to just rain money down on them. God doesn't have money in heaven. Jesus said it would come to us through man.

We deposit into the treasury of heaven by making our confession of faith over it. Then when we come to make a withdrawal from our heavenly account, we do it with our words. If you don't know what you desire, how will you be able to pray and get it? Ask yourself, "What is it that I need?"

Let's say you need a down payment to buy a house. You must lay hold on it in faith.

> **What things soever ye desire, when ye pray, believe that ye receive them, and ye shall have them.**
>
> **Mark 11:24**

Believe when you pray that you receive what you pray. You make deposits in heaven by faith. You also make withdrawals out of heaven by faith.

You put your money in your heavenly account by faith when you give it to man. Then you pull it out of your heavenly account by faith, and that withdrawal comes to you through man. Man is involved in the physical realm, but God is involved in the spiritual realm from the standpoint of the heart. When you give to God by giving to man, you worship Him with it. You receive your return from God by faith, through man.

God's Word says the heart of the king is in God's hand. (Prov. 21:1.) That means God can move on anyone. Don't limit God.

Some people do. They put limits on Him and expect their return to come through a certain person or in a certain way. That type of expectation causes frustration. Don't look to your job as your source, because if you do, you limit God. There are only so many hours you can work, only so much pay you can earn. That's the limit.

You remove the limits when you realize you aren't working for a living anymore; you're working for a giving. (Eph. 4:28.) God is vast and unlimited; therefore, you want to operate according to His system so you can tap into that unlimited realm.

When I work so that I have something to give, then the limits of financial increase are removed from me. The return can come to me from any direction.

When you fall in line with God, you have to lay hold in faith, saying, "I believe that I receive it."

> **For verily I say unto you, That whosoever shall say unto this mountain, Be thou removed, and be thou cast into the sea; and shall not doubt in his heart, but shall believe that those things which he saith shall come to pass; he shall have whatsoever he saith.**
>
> **Mark 11:23**

Faith is *in* the heart and *in* the mouth. Jesus said, "and shall not doubt in his heart." When Jesus referred to doubt in the heart, we often have the idea that He's talking about thoughts of doubt. But faith will still work, even when thoughts of doubt are running rampant in the mind. Remember, it says, "shall not doubt in his heart."

The word *doubt* is not referring to the way we think about doubt. Another word that could be placed here is "differ." That which is in your heart and in your mouth should not differ.

The biggest thing you have to do is get your heart and your mouth hooked up together. "Can two walk together, except they be agreed?" (Amos 3:3).

Many times we talk from our head or from our body, instead of from the Word of God.

> **Again I say unto you, That if two of you shall agree on earth as touching any thing that they shall ask, it shall be done for them of my Father which is in heaven.**
>
> **Matthew 18:19**

That does not mean I have to go and find someone to agree with, although it can mean that. It means I need to get my heart and mouth in agreement.

Remember, James 2:17 says that faith without works is dead. So you have to take some action that corresponds to what is in your heart and mouth.

You have a relationship with God, and the Spirit of God inside you will prompt you to do something. Actions will vary by what you're dealing with and by how God works with you.

This is a very personal thing. I can't take the way God works with me and tell you to operate by it. God may not deal with you in the same way that He deals with me because all faith is personal. We each have received salvation on our own faith. We put our own deposits in heaven by faith, and it has to be our own faith that we use to make withdrawals from our account.

3. Recognize the Enemy and Bind Him.

The third step is for you to recognize the enemy and bind him. In John 10:10 Jesus said, "The thief cometh not, but for to steal, and to kill, and to destroy: I am come that they might have life, and that they might have it more abundantly."

The thief is the devil and he wants to kill, steal, and destroy. He wants to steal this idea from you, to kill it, to destroy it. If he can destroy your faith, he can wear you down and cause you to feel hopeless. When you're hopeless, your faith won't work. You have to recognize the enemy and bind him.

> **Bring ye all the tithes into the storehouse, that there may be meat in mine house, and prove me now herewith, saith the Lord of hosts, if I will not open you the windows of heaven, and pour you out a blessing, that there shall not be room enough to receive it.**
>
> **And I will rebuke the devourer for your sakes....**
>
> **Malachi 3:10,11**

It will be hard for you to make withdrawals from your account if you don't make the right confession about your money when you deposit it into your heavenly account. When you make your deposit, be sure to include these statements in your confession:

- The devourer is rebuked.

- The windows of heaven are open.

- No weapon formed against me will prosper.

That's the confession Jesus will make to the Father in your behalf. Therefore, when you are in position to say, "I need my money out of heaven, and I believe I receive it now," the rebuking has already been done. You are already in position to take authority. You can confess:

"I affirm and confirm that which I said when I made my deposit; therefore, I know the devil is rebuked. I know he can't steal my seed. I know my blessings are on the way."

> **And these signs shall follow them that believe; In my name shall they cast out devils....**
>
> **Mark 16:17**

If the devil starts to work in some area concerning what you are believing God for, then you can start speaking in the name of Jesus to the spiritual strong man that's involved. Rebuke him. Remind him, "You have no place in this! I'm a tither!"

First, you decide; you lay hold in faith, and then you recognize the enemy and bind him. Remember, "Whatsoever ye shall bind on earth shall be bound in heaven" (Matt. 18:18). Put a stop to the devil's maneuvering, by your confession, by your prayer, and by the declaration of your faith.

4. Loose the Forces of Heaven.

Step four in making withdrawals involves the ministry of angels. In Hebrews the apostle Paul said this about angels:

> **But to which of the angels said he at any time, Sit on my right hand, until I make thine enemies thy footstool?**
>
> **Are they not all ministering spirits, sent forth to minister for them who shall be heirs of salvation?**
>
> **Hebrews 1:13,14**

We are heirs of salvation, and the ministering spirits are there to minister for us.

You make your confession by saying something like this: "My God is supplying all my need, so I believe I receive my need met."

Specify exactly what the needs are in your life. Then God will work to meet those needs. The angels have been sent to minister in your behalf by speaking to and moving in man's heart.

You can expect money to come because you have given. You have laid your treasure in heaven. You have made your confession. You believe that the blessings of God are overtaking you. You can have what you say. (Mark 11:23.) There is certainty to it.

> The Lord hath prepared his throne in the heavens; and his kingdom ruleth over all.
>
> Bless the Lord, ye his angels, that excel in strength, that do his commandments, hearkening unto the voice of his word.
>
> Psalm 103:19,20

Angels will speak what they have heard the Spirit of God say. You have made your confession and are holding fast to it, so the angels say those same things to people in your behalf. Your treasures will be pulled out of your heavenly account.

Psalm 103:21 says, "Bless ye the Lord, all ye his hosts; ye ministers of his, that do his pleasure." God takes pleasure in the prosperity of His servants. It pleases God for you to receive money from your heavenly account.

This might make those who don't understand it angry. You will have to put up with persecutions, but you can still be happy in God.

Realize that other people can't stop the blessings of God from coming to you. Those people may get in the way. They may hinder, but they can't stop God's work in your life. And they won't hinder it for too long, because "If God be for us, who can be against us?" (Rom. 8:31).

The last step in making a withdrawal from your heavenly account is to praise God for the answer.

5. Praise God for the Answer.

Start glorifying and praising God with words like these:

"Thank You, Lord, for supplying my every need. I've made the necessary deposits in my heavenly account, so now I praise You for the answer. The money is on the way to meet my needs, so I believe I receive. Glory be to God!"

You can just keep on rejoicing in the Holy Spirit. When you praise God like this, it sets off something within you, because you are pleasing to Him. The joy of the Lord becomes your strength. (Neh. 8:10.) You have given in faith and withdrawn in faith, and you have a confident and favorable expectation, knowing that your supply is on its way.

8

PLANNING FOR MONEY

Do you know any Christians who stand by their mailboxes waiting for the Publishers Clearing House Sweepstakes entry form? We often laugh at this, yet there is a sad truth here.

Today people are looking to win the "big one," the lottery, the raffle, bingo, or the big giveaway. They see forms of gambling as the way to fulfill their dreams. Some people who live on welfare payments are spending their money on lottery tickets. Seniors on fixed incomes use their time and money to play bingo. Many people can't pay their bills because they have squandered their money trying to hit the "big one."

> *God intends for money to be your tool, not your dictator.*

> Retirement isn't
> mentioned in
> the Bible.

Maybe you have heard the believer who tells his pastor, "When I win the lottery, Pastor, I'll give 10 percent to the church." Nonsense! If he doesn't tithe off of $100 a week, he will never tithe on $10 million, because he doesn't have money. Money has him.

Money will always have control of your life if you are looking to money as your source. As I pointed out at the beginning of this study, God intends for money to be your tool, not your dictator.

Too often I have heard people say, "If I could just win the lottery or the sweepstakes or play the market, I would retire." But there's a problem with this plan. People have a wrong attitude about work and money. They have lost sight of this fundamental truth in God's law. God expects us to work. Man was never created for a life of idleness or nonproductivity.

I know my next statement will shock some people, but it's true. Retirement isn't mentioned in the Bible. The type and amount of work we do will change as we age, but God still expects us to work. In fact, I don't plan to retire; I'm just going to re-fire.

Let's look at an effective plan for money.

PART 1: HOW TO GET MONEY — GO TO WORK

Man is expected to work to obtain finances. You may say, "But I thought work was a curse." God gave us work to bless us. Work is cursed only if you're out of position or place, or if you're working for a living rather than working for a giving.

God works, and we are made in His image. Work began in the Garden of Eden when God gave Adam work to do.

> **And God blessed them, and God said unto them, Be fruitful, and multiply, and replenish the earth, and subdue it: and have dominion over the fish of the sea, and over the fowl of the air, and over every living thing that moveth upon the earth.**
>
> **Genesis 1:28**

> **And out of the ground the Lord God formed every beast of the field, and every fowl of the air; and brought them unto Adam to see what he would call them: and whatsoever Adam called every living creature, that was the name thereof.**
>
> **And Adam gave names to all cattle, and to the fowl of the air, and to every beast of the field; but for Adam there was not found an help meet for him.**
>
> **Genesis 2:19,20**

And with that labor came reward: Adam would have food to eat as a result. (Gen. 1:29,30.) Work was cursed when Adam sinned. (Gen. 3:17-19.) Work would never again be as it was for Adam in the Garden. Sin changed humanity.

Then Jesus came and redeemed us from the curse of the law. (Gal. 3:13.) That redemption doesn't mean we don't work anymore. Jesus got rid of the curse, not work.

Work allows us to bless our families, employers or employees, and others. As we exchange our time, talent, and energy for money, we can give back to God in the form of tithes, offerings, and alms. Then the gospel goes forth, and lives are changed as people are saved and become disciples of the Lord.

As we work, we do our part to provide for our family's needs and for the needs of others. We do what we can to meet our needs, always recognizing that God is our Source. Then God does His part to make up the difference. As it says in 1 Corinthians 3:9, "We are labourers together with God."

Galatians 2:20 says we live by faith in the Son of God. Some people have taken this Scripture out of context and have used it as an excuse for their laziness. They say, "I'm living by faith." Living by faith doesn't mean you don't work.

The book of Proverbs is the Book of Wisdom, and it repeatedly makes reference to work and the diligent person. It tells us that the hand of the diligent makes rich. (Prov. 10:4.) A diligent man is faithful, persevering, and responsible. (Prov.

27:23-27.) Consequently, one who is diligent is a blessed and prosperous person. His family and friends are blessed. His community is blessed.

Proverbs 31 extols the godly, hardworking woman. This woman's godliness and diligence produces blessing for her entire household.

The apostle Paul told the thief to steal no more: "...but rather let him labour, working with his hands the thing which is good, that he may have to give to him that needeth" (Eph. 4:28). Paul expected people to work for a giving.

We work for a giving because we live and move and have our being in Christ Jesus. (Acts 17:28.) We work to give.

Paul made tents although he preached the gospel and was an apostle to many churches in Greece and Asia Minor. He labored both in the gospel and in a trade. Jesus worked as a carpenter before He began to minister. Among the twelve disciples were businessmen, a tax collector, fishermen, and so on.

Neither Jesus nor any New Testament writer preached against work. Instead, the Bible warns us against laziness and slothfulness in every area of our lives. The book of Proverbs graphically depicts the fate of a slothful man. The one who won't diligently and faithfully work and provide for his family is condemned to lack and want. And he brings that curse upon his children.

In 1 Timothy 5:8, Paul described the person who won't provide for others, especially his own family, as "worse than an infidel."

So it's vital that we work. That way we obtain money to operate God's financial plan, which is the second way we obtain money.

Second, man is expected to believe God and to obey His Word. In other words, we are expected to operate God's heavenly banking system, which has been explained in previous chapters.

No matter how much we work, we will never have enough money to meet every need or to satisfy every desire. We can only work so many hours in the day or week. There will always be more that we want or need. We can't work our way entirely out of debt. The only way to meet every need and desire and to get completely out of debt is to believe God and to operate His financial system. We must therefore believe that God is the Lord of increase, and we must understand and practice His principles for increase.

Working the principle is law, and a certain measure of increase will come that way. The greatest increase comes because of our relationship with God. When we seek first God and His righteousness, and believe the Lord to honor His Word, the increase will come.

Believing God for money isn't a formula; it's a lifestyle. It is a willingness to hear God and to allow Him to correct our attitudes and actions.

If we believe God for money, we have to listen to Him as to where, when, and how we are to give and to spend the money. We must give it and spend it according to His will. If we are willing to be obedient in the short term, we will be blessed in the long term.

Fellowship, communion with Him, and obedience to His voice are the results when we trust Him. If we are faithful to do this, we will have victory in our finances.

Another way to obtain money is to put your money to work for you by investing in the natural realm. Your money is already working for you in the supernatural realm when you pay tithes and give offerings. As I said earlier, the natural rules for money management and investing are beyond the scope of this book. But I want you to realize that you don't have to overwork yourself, hold down two or three jobs, and neglect your family to have money. Your money can work for you. Learn to take the extra, even if it is a small amount, and put it to work for you.

PART 2: MANAGING MONEY

Managing your money has both supernatural and natural aspects. You need both aspects, but the supernatural is by far the most important.

The supernatural aspect is allowing God to be Lord of your finances. When you accepted Jesus as Savior, that meant you also accepted Him as Lord. If He is to be your Lord, then He has to be Lord of your finances, too. You must allow Him to lead you in managing your money.

A common mistake people make is to spend all their money. Acquiring wealth means learning to manage money. You have to make your money work for you.

When you're young, you have more time than money. As you grow older, you should have more money than time. Learn to make money work for you; then you can use your time more wisely.

When it comes to money management, many fail to distinguish between their wants and their needs. Everything is a "need" when we think a "want" is a need. But a "want" is something unnecessary, something we can wait on.

As you spend time with God, you will learn the difference between your wants and your needs. Then you will discover you can trust God for all of it, rather than go into debt.

A choice to go into debt for our wants will eventually cause trouble when it comes to paying for our needs. Our most vital need is to pay our tithes, give offerings, and give alms. The deeper we go into debt, the less we have to give. Therefore, we're no longer working for a giving; we're working to pay for our wants.

THE INSTANT GRATIFICATION TRAP

Instant gratification is a trap to get you to quit believing God. It makes you the lord of your finances and the provider of your needs and wants, rather than allowing God to fill this place in your life. If you don't believe Jesus will provide your needs and wants, you will have to look to the bank, to friends and relatives, and to your credit cards to be your provider.

Now, there is nothing wrong with credit, but you must be disciplined to manage your money and make it work for you. If you can't discipline yourself to commune daily with God and hear His voice concerning your finances, you certainly don't need credit. Credit can disable your ability to distinguish between wants and needs. If you allow God to be Lord of your finances, you will not end up in debt.

Your income represents your life. Therefore, if you don't pay your tithes or give offerings and alms, you are telling God you can manage your own life, rather than allowing Him to lead by His Spirit.

A vital part of managing your money is managing yourself. You might ask, "Now, what does managing myself have to do with managing my money?" You trade your time, talent, and energy for money. You actually "cash in" a part of your life for money.

The common mistake many make is that they fail to figure their worth when it comes to managing money. As you manage your income, you will discover that certain expenditures are really investments. For example, clothes for your job, reliable transportation to get yourself to work, and money for continuing education are investments. You're investing in yourself and your ability to earn money for a giving. The more you earn, the more you have to give.

Ask yourself before you spend money, "What's the return for this amount that I'm going to spend? What value does this expenditure have in my life?" As you answer these questions, it will help you make quality decisions concerning your expenditures.

You will grow into more comfortable margins with your income and outflow as you learn to manage your money. You will have extra. Then you should begin to invest in the future. As you do, remember to value your time.

> *You defeat the purpose of God's blessings in your life when you don't count your worth.*

We assume that only poor people have poverty spirits, but that isn't so. Wealthy people can have a poverty mentality because gaining and keeping money has become their life.

A poverty spirit will also manifest as an unwillingness to spend money to get things done. People with this kind of spirit assume that hiring someone to get things done is a waste of money. Instead, they spend their own time doing those things.

If you're young, you will have more time than money, so you will probably have to do those jobs. When you are older your time becomes more valuable, and there may be more productive things you should be doing.

You defeat the purpose of God's blessings in your life when you don't count your worth. Now, it isn't wrong to do things for yourself, such as mowing the lawn, painting the house, or working on the car. If you enjoy those things, then don't worry about it.

When God has prospered you, do you continue to do such things just so you won't have to pay someone else to do them? Are you becoming greedy and stingy? Are you more concerned about keeping money than obeying God?

God blesses us so that we can spend quality time with Him and with our families, and be witnesses for Him. If you're consumed with money and don't manage it to your benefit, you will spend all of your time working. Then you won't have any time for God or for your family.

Your family may hear you say, "God is my Source," but then they watch you spend every waking moment working for a dollar. Learn to manage your time as well as your money.

Time is the only resource you can't save. You can only spend it. When godly prosperity comes, don't discount the blessing of extra time. When you've managed your money, you will have time to spend with your family and God. Your immediate needs will be met and, to a large extent, so will your wants.

When the blessings of God flow, be a wise steward. You will have the time to be a blessing to your loved ones. Take advantage of the opportunity.

PART 3: PLANNING FOR YOUR FINANCIAL FUTURE

Preparation for your financial future has both supernatural and natural aspects to it. Let's discuss the supernatural side.

We've mentioned that you have to determine to be a tither and a giver. The fundamentals of paying tithe and giving have been covered in previous chapters. The key is to be a cheerful giver who expects a return.

Many people fall into a common trap as they become financially comfortable. They no longer "name" their seed or expect a return. In the process of accumulating wealth, living off of 90 percent of your income becomes easy. The true stretch is to set a target to give more.

R.G. LeTourneau said, "The question is not how much of my money I give to God, but rather how much of God's money I keep for myself."[1] By the end of his life, he was giving 90 percent of his income for the Lord's work and living off 10 percent.[2] That's a goal to shoot for.

You might wonder, *But what about me? Could I ever do that?*

Well, it depends. Supernaturally managing your money requires your faith and discipline as an individual. If you're married, it requires agreement between you and your spouse. I will use my wife and myself as an example.

Over the years, Pat and I have developed a relationship of mutual trust. In the beginning years, we agreed upon a set amount above our tithes that we could give without consulting one another. I could give what God told me to give without consulting her, and she could do the same. When the amount of the offering exceeded the predetermined figure, we would consult with one another before we gave or pledged that amount. This kept us in harmony and made our prayers effective.

As our finances have increased, so has the amount we can give without consulting one another. This arrangement has given us the freedom to plant seeds separate of one another but always in agreement.

The point is, Pat and I are in agreement. We pray at the start of each year concerning direction for that year. Our prayer includes direction concerning our giving.

As husband and wife, we have set our hearts toward God. We want to obey Him in how much, where, and when we should give. We can't prosper if we aren't in tune with God's plan for our lives. Randomly scattering seed isn't God's best plan. Of course, we will pray about our offerings all year long, but asking God for direction at the beginning of each year establishes His priorities above our own.

Another vital key to the supernatural side of your financial future is to choose the ground where you will sow your seed.

Don't give to ministries and individuals you don't believe in. Your faith is mixed with your seed. If you have no faith in that particular ground, you will be wasting your time; your seed just won't produce. I have seen ministers sow into their own churches or ministries while bad-mouthing their own financial partners. And their seeds don't produce because they curse the givers.

As you listen to God concerning your giving, He will direct you to stretch your giving. He wants you to do more and to expect Him to do more for you. Tithing protects your seed and opens the windows of heaven. But if you want to experience an abundant harvest, you have to give offerings and alms, gifts that exceed your tithes. The more you need, the more you'll have to give.

Sometimes the Lord may tell you to stop giving to a particular ministry or individual. Maybe there is something going on that you don't know about. Maybe the Lord wants to fine-tune your hearing to His voice. Or it could be that He doesn't want your giving to become a routine habit that's stale and lifeless. Habits are good; just don't become lazy in your listening to God.

In everything you do with God, you must do it with your whole heart. God has given promises concerning tithes, offerings, and alms. He has given you the power to get wealth, in the present and future. The responsibility falls upon you to hear His commands. It's a matter of discipline and commitment, allowing your relationship with Him to remain vital and vibrant, stretching yourself at His command.

Let's turn our attention now to some things we need to be doing in the natural realm. Ideally, if all of us had begun saving and investing when we were eighteen years of age, we would be financially secure when we reached the senior years of our lives. But it doesn't matter how old we are; the important thing is for us to begin saving and investing now.

We all have a responsibility to take part in caring for ourselves and our loved ones. The current worldly mentality is "Let the government take care of me." But God never intended for our government to have that job.

As Christians, we are to trust and believe in God and to do all we know to do in the natural to prepare for our senior years. At the same time, the Lord admonishes us to leave a blessing to our children and to our grandchildren. (Prov. 13:22.) He isn't talking about a mortgage or credit card debt that will take three generations to pay off.

In the illustration below, you will see the general guidelines for the beginning investor.

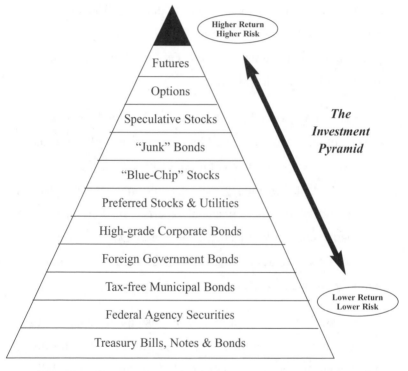

A major key to investing is setting goals and sticking to them. Start with investing in yourself. Set a goal that you will put at least 10 percent of your income into savings, just as you tithe 10 percent. Then as your ability to increase your giving goes up, you should increase the amount you set aside for yourself.

God wants us to be a blessing to others, but He also blesses us. We are to be wise stewards of those blessings.

Often Christians won't read, study, or educate themselves about investment plans, savings plans, or life insurance plans. This is wrong. It isn't a lack of faith to plan ahead. If we aren't to plan for the future, why would God admonish us to provide for our children and grandchildren? God wouldn't tell us to do something He considers wrong.

Have an open mind about investing. Read and study what you can on it. Go to seminars. Many community colleges offer courses on money management for a relatively inexpensive fee. Numerous books on money management and financial planning are available. Talk to financial experts. And don't just talk to Christian ones; talk to secular experts, too. Don't be afraid to ask questions or to admit your ignorance. Then take the information you have gained and go to God in prayer.

You don't manage your money by wishing or hoping. One young man came to me for advice some time ago. It seems his money management system consisted of stuffing all of his bills into a drawer and pretending they weren't there. But of course, that didn't work. No matter how much he ignored them, bills continued to mount, and all the creditors still wanted payment. You can't ignore money management and, at the same time, expect to prosper.

Budget and management are not anti-faith words. God tells us in His Word to plan and to count the cost. (Luke 14:28.) And He expects us to do it.

THE "END OF THE EARTH" SYNDROME

Sadly though, there are some in the body of Christ who live in the "end of the earth" syndrome. It goes something like this: "I won't pay off my car, or my house, or my credit cards. I'll just keep making the payments and stay current because I know the Lord is returning."

These people never know financial freedom because they live in bondage to the lender. When an attack comes, like the loss of a job, or sickness, or even the death of a mate, they can be wiped out financially.

"But God would never allow that," they say. And they're right. He wouldn't. They are the ones who allow it by living for the moment and satisfying their wants, rather than obeying God. They aren't trusting Him.

Now, don't misunderstand me. There is no sin in owing money. You can owe money, but you're in trouble when you can't repay it. So, get on top of your financial life, and plan for your financial future.

Don't get caught in the "I know" syndrome. Knowing is not doing. Start planning. If you're married, get in agreement with your mate. If you're single, get in agreement with a friend or your pastor. Ask yourself some hard questions: What is a "want"? What is a "need"? Are we living beyond our means? Can we cut back? If so, where?

By reading this book, you are learning the principles that Pat and I have applied in our lives. But our prosperity didn't happen overnight. It's been the result of years of stewardship and obedience to the God who is faithful to His Word. We have studied to show ourselves approved and have applied what we have learned. (2 Tim. 2:15.)

With great wealth comes great responsibility and great temptation. You want the wealth now. At the age of thirty you want what your parents earned at age sixty-five. But are you ready for the responsibility and the temptation that comes with the increase?

Your responsibility is to obey God in your giving. The more you have to give, the more He will ask you to give. The temptation in becoming prosperous is to forget the Lord your God.

The only way you can be ready for the responsibility and capable of overcoming the temptation is by submitting yourself to God, to His Word, and to His ways. If you will manage the little that you have now, He will give you more to manage. When you have submitted to Him and learned to manage what He has given you, then and only then will you be ready for more.

Remember God's warning to the Old Testament people in Deuteronomy 8. This still applies to us today.

> **Beware that thou forget not the Lord thy God, in not keeping his commandments, and his judgments, and his statutes, which I command thee this day:**
>
> **Lest when thou hast eaten and art full, and hast built goodly houses, and dwelt therein;**
>
> **And when thy herds and thy flocks multiply, and thy silver and thy gold is multiplied, and all that thou hast is multiplied;**
>
> **Then thine heart be lifted up, and thou forget the Lord thy God, which brought thee forth out of the land of Egypt, from the house of bondage;**
>
> **Who led thee through that great and terrible wilderness, wherein were fiery serpents, and scorpions, and drought, where there was no water; who brought thee forth water out of the rock of flint;**
>
> **Who fed thee in the wilderness with manna, which thy fathers knew not, that he might humble thee, and that he might prove thee, to do thee good at thy latter end;**
>
> **And thou say in thine heart, My power and the might of mine hand hath gotten me this wealth.**
>
> **But thou shalt remember the Lord thy God: for it is he that giveth thee power to get wealth, that he may establish his covenant which he sware unto thy fathers, as it is this day.**

And it shall be, if thou do at all forget the Lord thy God, and walk after other gods, and serve them, and worship them, I testify against you this day that ye shall surely perish.

Deuteronomy 8:11-19

9

REVELATION, CONSISTENCY, AND CONFESSION

by Pat Harrison

Buddy and I were very young when we married; I was seventeen, and he was nineteen. We loved God and were born again, and I knew the voice of God from an early age; but we didn't have much knowledge.

Buddy handled the checkbook then. Sometimes he would pay tithes, and sometimes he wouldn't. It depended on how much money we had. We were inconsistent in giving our tithes for two reasons. We hadn't been properly taught, and we had some religious thinking that says, "If you can't pay bills, God doesn't expect you to pay tithes." After we received some revelation, we realized that we needed to pay tithes so we could pay our bills. But as I said, we were young and inexperienced.

Since we were inconsistent in giving our tithes, sometimes we had money, and sometimes we didn't. But when Buddy fully submitted himself to following God, things began to change. He became consistent in everything — tithes, offerings, prayers, study of the Word. Good things began to consistently happen for us.

We understood the importance of the tithes, but we still didn't have a revelation about tithing, the confession. When we gained understanding of tithing and began to make our confession concerning our tithes, things got even better. We began to say what the Word says about the tither. We proclaimed we had tither's rights, that God opens the windows of heaven for us and pours out blessings, and that the devourer is rebuked.

> *First, we got the revelation. Then we consistently acted on the revelation, and the blessings began overtaking us.*

The more Buddy and I studied the Word and asked questions of our pastor, Leonard Wood, and my father, Kenneth Hagin, the more revelation we got concerning offerings and giving to the poor, the rest of God's banking system, although we didn't call it a banking system at that time. We realized that we were to give offerings and give to the poor, besides giving our tithes, and that we were to speak God's Word concerning our offerings, too.

We believed God that our seed was planted in good ground, that it would reap in abundance to the best of its capabilities, and that it would harvest at the right time. That is what we spoke over our offerings. We looked for opportunities to give and joyfully planted wherever the Lord directed, which I continue to do and will do until Jesus comes!

First, we got the revelation. Then we consistently acted on the revelation, and the blessings began overtaking us.

Our publishing companies and our ministry tithe and give offerings because we believe in the principle of giving tithes, offerings, and giving to the poor. I know people will say, "Well, the Bible doesn't say that churches or ministries or businesses have to tithe or give." Yes, I know the Bible does not require churches or ministries or businesses to tithe and give. But giving is a principle all through the Word of God because God is a giver. It's about being blessed to be a blessing and allowing the blessings of God to flow through you to others. It's about loving God.

When businesses and ministries tithe and give offerings, then they can claim tither's rights and the promises connected with giving offerings and giving to the poor. They can expect to prosper. How can a church or ministry ask its members or partners to tithe and give offerings if the church or ministry doesn't do that? I believe we are to practice what we preach. We experienced double blessings because we personally tithed and gave offerings and our ministry and businesses did. I continue to do so today personally, through the ministry, and through businesses.

GOD'S BANKING SYSTEM

In the late 70s and early 80s, strong teaching on faith came forth: believing God and understanding who you are in God and that your faith in God and in His Word is what produces everything you need; what God said is yours. That teaching was vital and important then and still is today. It is truth, but some people took the faith teaching to the extreme. They interpreted "living by faith" to mean that they didn't need to have retirement plans, savings accounts, or insurance.

God gives us common sense, a brain, and intelligence, and He expects us to use them. When the faith teaching first came forth, many people forgot about common sense and intelligence. They got rid of their savings accounts, retirement plans, car insurance, and health insurance.

Buddy was concerned about that situation. He understood the practical, natural principles concerning prosperity, and he understood and practiced faith and the Word of God. As a pastor, he wanted to help Christians find the truth and walk in it. He went to God and to the Word. He studied and prayed, and that is when God gave him the revelation concerning His banking system and how a greater, supernatural prosperity would come to a Christian who operated in God's system and the world's system with biblical ethics.

As Buddy taught this in our church and around the world, so many people told us how the teaching brought them understanding and revelation. People told us they had been giving their tithes but hadn't seen it working for them as they had expected. When they began to confess over their tithes and offerings, they saw greater returns.

There had been very little teaching on giving to the poor at that time, so what Buddy taught was vital. I believe that even today many people still don't really understand the blessed opportunity to give to the poor and how God repays that loan. We often think that if we give clothes or food, that is exactly what we will get back. And we do, but that is not all. Giving to the poor is bestowing favor, kindness, and compassion upon others. Consequently, favor, kindness, and compassion come back to us in many ways. We may not even recognize that the good coming to us is a result of giving to the poor. God is a compassionate and kind God, and He's going to repay exceedingly, abundantly above what we can imagine.

I can say today that I am a blessed woman because I pay my tithes, give offerings, and give to the poor. I have a beautiful home and all that I need. I am very blessed. I look at God's blessings every day and thank Him for them. I also realize that all I have are things, and not one of those blessings has me. If God told me to walk out of my home today, I would joyfully do it because I know God is my Source. He's the God of abundance. And He never goes backward; He always moves forward. I can walk away from something today because I know He will give me something much better tomorrow. He is consistent in His love, mercy, grace, and goodness toward me; therefore, I choose to be consistent with Him.

The Bible says we are in this world but not of this world. (John 17:15.) That means we are not exempt from the laws of the land because we live in the land. But we are exempt from the enemy's attacks on us in this land because our citizenship is in heaven. We overcome by staying in righteousness with God and by going forth and practicing the principles of His Word. The temptations, tests, trials, and even crises, will come, but we walk through them in victory because of Jesus and His blood.

Let me encourage you to study the Scriptures that Buddy used in this book. Don't hold onto religious thinking or man's traditions or interpretations. Choose to hear the Lord and obey His voice.

Will you have temptations, tests, and trials when you practice God's banking system? Of course; the devil will try to steal the Word. He doesn't want you to obey God because he knows that is your victory and his defeat. But when you know God and you know that you are following to the fullest of your ability that which He has called you to do, then you will have what God says. I am living proof.

My prayer for those who read this book is that they will understand that prosperity is a godly principle and they will gain knowledge and understanding to walk in it.

As you read and reread this book, ask the Lord to reveal by His Holy Spirit these truths to you. With God and His revelation, all things are possible! Dig out these truths, and move into God's abundant blessings.

God bless you.

Triumphantly Always in Christ,
Pat Harrison

TITHING THE TITHE —
YOUR CONFESSIONS

Father God, we thank You for the lordship and deity of Jesus. He is Your Son and our Savior, our Healer, our Provider. He is the Apostle of our faith, the High Priest of our confession; and it is in Him, Father, that we lift our tithes unto You.

Lord Jesus, take our tithes and worship the Father with them. We declare that the devourer is rebuked and the windows of heaven are opened, for we profess this day unto the Lord God that we have come into our inheritance that the Lord swore to give us. We are in the land that You have provided for us in Jesus Christ, the kingdom of Almighty God.

Jesus, Lord and High Priest, we bring the firstfruits of our income to You and worship the Lord our God with it. We rejoice in all the good that You have given to us and our household. We have listened to the voice of the Lord our God and have done according to all that He has commanded us. Now look down from Your holy habitation from heaven and bless us as You said in Your Word. As You worship the Father with our tithes, we set our hearts to receive a hundredfold return.

Father God, because Christ is alive in our lives, we have power to bind Satan and to loose the blessings of God. Therefore, you foul spirits of poverty, lack, and debt, we bind you in the name of Jesus. You cannot work in our spirits, our minds, our bodies, our marriage, our family, our business, our finances, or our social activities. You foul spirits are bound in Jesus' name.

Spirit of prosperity, we loose you in the name of Jesus to work in our spirits, our minds, our bodies, our marriage, our family, our business, our finances, and our social activities. Spirit of prosperity, you are loosed to do us good in all areas of our lives.

Father God, You have blessed us with the blessings of the Lord. We are blessed when we go out and blessed when we come in. We are blessed in the field and blessed in the store. Everything we put our hands to is blessed. Now, we don't run after these blessings; these blessings are running after us and overtaking us because You have made us the head and not the tail. We are born from above and not from beneath. Our enemies come against us one way and flee seven. Goodness and mercy follow us all the days of our lives. In Jesus' name, amen.

(Titus 1:4; Exodus 15:26; Genesis 22:14; Hebrews 3:1; Mark 4:20, 10:29,30; Matthew 16:19; Deuteronomy 28:1-4; Psalm 23:6.)

SCRIPTURES FOR
FURTHER STUDY

In God's kingdom, we have a wonderful inheritance. Part of that inheritance is prosperity in every area of our lives — spirit, soul, and body. The focus of this book is on financial prosperity and God's banking system. God desires that we enter into prosperity and wealth through the operation of His principles. This isn't a complete list of Scriptures, but it is a starting point for your study.

INHERITANCE

Genesis 26:1-4

Psalm 37:34

Proverbs 8:17-21

Proverbs 17:2

Proverbs 20:21

Ezekiel 46:16-18

Luke 15:11-31

INVESTMENTS

Genesis 26:12-14

Proverbs 21:20

Proverbs 24:27

Matthew 6:19-21

Matthew 13:22

Matthew 25:14-30

Luke 14:28,29

Luke 19:13-26

2 Peter 3:10

TITHES

Genesis 14:18-23

Deuteronomy 14:22,28

Proverbs 3:9,10

Malachi 3:10

Matthew 23:23

Hebrews 7:1,2,4,5,8

OFFERINGS

Exodus 25:1,2

Exodus 35:4,5,21,22,29

Exodus 36:5-7

1 Samuel 9:6-8 (to man of God)

1 Kings 17:14-16

1 Chronicles 29:1,3,9

Psalm 96:7,8

Proverbs 11:24-26

Ecclesiates 11:1

Luke 6:38

Luke 21:1-4

1 Corinthians 9:9-11,14

2 Corinthians 8:7,8,11-15

2 Corinthians 9:6-11

Galatians 6:6-10

GIVING TO THE POOR

Psalm 72:12-14

Psalm 109:31

Proverbs 3:27

Proverbs 19:17

Proverbs 22:9

Matthew 5:42

Matthew 10:42

Luke 3:11

Luke 10:35

Luke 12:33

Luke 19:8,9

Acts 20:32-35

1 Corinthians 16:1,2

1 Timothy 5:8

NEED

Psalm 37:25

Matthew 6:8,25-33

Philippians 4:19

SAVINGS

Proverbs 6:6-8

Proverbs 21:20

Proverbs 30:24,25

LAZINESS

Proverbs 6:6-11

Proverbs 12:24

Proverbs 13:11

Proverbs 14:4

Proverbs 21:17

Ephesians 4:28

2 Thessalonians 3:10

SLOTHFULNESS

Haggai 1:5,6

Proverbs 18:9

Proverbs 24:30,31

Ecclesiastes 10:18

2 Thessalonians 3:11

Hebrews 6:12

WASTE

Genesis 41:36

Luke 15:13

John 6:12

PROSPERITY

Genesis 39:3

Deuteronomy 28:11-13

Deuteronomy 29:9

Joshua 1:8

2 Chronicles 31:21

Psalm 1:3

Psalm 30:5,6

Psalm 34:9,10

Psalm 35:27

Proverbs 10:22

Proverbs 28:13

Isaiah 1:19

Jeremiah 17:7,8

Luke 6:38

John 10:10

2 Corinthians 8:9

Philippians 4:19

3 John 2

WEALTH

Deuteronomy 8

Proverbs 10:22

Isaiah 32:8

Luke 12:16-21

ACCOUNTING

Daniel 6:1-3

Matthew 18:21-35

Matthew 25:14-30

Romans 14:12

FAITHFUL

Psalm 101:6

1 Corinthians 4:1,2

ENDNOTES

Chapter 1

[1] Bennett, 253.

[2] Moffat.

[3] Strong, 54, #3520.

[4] Ibid., #2428.

[5] Vidal, 343.

[6] Davies, 27.

[7] *The Oxford Dictionary and Thesaurus.*

[8] Davies, 13.

Chapter 2

[1] *Vines Expository Dictionary of Old and New Testament Words,* 132-133. *The Oxford Dictionary and Thesaurus,* 143-144.

[2] *The Oxford Dictionary and Thesaurus,* 475.

Chapter 3

[1] Strong, 70, #4643.

[2] Ibid., #2431.

[3] *The Spirit Filled Life Bible,* 1762.

[4] *The Oxford Dictionary and Thesaurus,* 692.

[5] Woodbridge, 340-343.

[6] Ibid., 344-349.

[7] Ibid., 351.

Chapter 4

[1] Strong, #2431.

[2] *The Oxford Dictionary and Thesaurus.*

Chapter 5

[1] Strong, 113, #7706.

[2] Ibid., 41, #2603.

[3] Ibid., 30 #1800.

[4] Ibid., 90 #5041.

[5] Ibid., 107, #7326.

[6] Ibid., 59, #3867.

Chapter 8

[1] Woodbridge, 349.

[2] Ibid.

REFERENCES

Bennett, William J. *Our Sacred Honor.* Nashville, TN: Broadman and Holman Publishers, 1997.

Davies, Glyn. *A History of Money.* Cardiff, Wales: University of Wales Press, 1994.

Moffat, James. *The Bible. A New Translation.* New York: Harper & Row, 1954.

Strong, James. *The New Strong's Exhaustive Concordance of the Bible.* Nashville: Thomas Nelson Publishers, 1990.

The Oxford Dictionary and Thesaurus. Oxford, CT: Oxford University Press, 1996.

The Spirit Filled Life Bible, Nashville: Thomas Nelson Publishers, 1991.

Vidal, Gore. *Lincoln.* New York: Random House, Inc., 1984.

Vines Expository Dictionary of Old and New Testament Words. Old Tappan, NJ: Fleming H. Revell Company, 1981.

Woodbridge, John. *More than Conquerors.* Chicago: Moody Press, 1992.

ABOUT THE AUTHOR

DR. DOYLE "BUDDY" HARRISON

By discipline and training you will receive more; and by being faithful and obedient, God will impart even more, so that you can fulfill the leadership position God has called you to.

— Buddy Harrison

Buddy Harrison, along with his wife, Pat, were co-founders of Faith Christian Fellowship International Church. He served as president of the organization from 1978 until he went home to be with the Lord on November 28, 1998. The Lord instructed Buddy to be a pastor to pastors and ministers, providing guidance for them in the spiritual and natural realms. FCF International is in relationship with more than 1000 churches and 2000 ministers globally. Its programs include Credentialing for Ministers, Affiliation and Association of Churches, Strategic Planning, Family Care Center, Legal Advice, Accounting Consultation, On-site Management Consultation, Stewardship Services, and International Mission Program. It partners with The Life Link for humanitarian outreach. Dr. Harrison strongly believed in the value of covenant relationships and walking under authority, and he set the example for the FCF family. Today under the leadership of Pat Harrison, FCF continues to foster solid covenant relationships around the world among its ministers and churches.

As the co-founder and chairman of Harrison House Publishers, Buddy obeyed God's vision to provide ministers a vehicle by which to put their message into print. Harrison House has become the largest charismatic book publisher, with markets in more than 180 countries and publishing translations in 49 languages. What began with a few family members and close friends now employs more than 200 associates and has created new companies, including Albury Publishing, Honor Books, RiverOak Publishing, Access Sales International, and Life Impact Books.

Buddy Harrison successfully incorporated his knowledge and skills of the corporate world with the Lord's calling on his life. As an anointed teacher and astute businessman, he traveled the world sharing these steps to success and favor.

To contact Mrs. Pat Harrison
write:

Faith Christian Fellowship International Church, Inc.
P.O. Box 35443
Tulsa, OK 74153-0443
918-492-5800
Website: www.fcf.org

Please include your prayer requests
and comments when you write.

OTHER BOOKS BY
<u>BUDDY HARRISON</u>

Count It All Joy (co-authored by Van Gale)

Four Keys to Power

Getting in Position to Receive

How to Raise Your Kids in Troubled Times

Just Do It

Maintaining a Spirit-Filled Life

Man, Husband, Father

Petitioning for the Impossible

Seven Steps to a Quality Decision

The Force of Mercy (co-authored by Dr. Michael Landsman)

Understanding Authority for Effective Leadership

Understanding Spiritual Gifts

PRAYER OF SALVATION

A born-again, committed relationship with God is the key to a victorious life. Jesus, the Son of God, laid down His life and rose again so that we could spend eternity with Him in heaven and experience His absolute best on earth. The Bible says, "For God so loved the world, that he gave his only begotten Son, that whosoever believeth in him should not perish, but have everlasting life" (John 3:16).

It is the will of God that everyone receive eternal salvation. The way to receive this salvation is to call upon the name of Jesus and confess Him as your Lord. The Bible says, "That if thou shalt confess with thy mouth the Lord Jesus, and shalt believe in thine heart that God hath raised him from the dead, thou shalt be saved. For whosoever shall call upon the name of the Lord shall be saved" (Rom. 10:9,13).

Jesus has given salvation, healing, and countless benefits to all who call upon His name. These benefits can be yours if you receive Him into your heart by praying this prayer:

Heavenly Father, I come to You admitting that I am a sinner. Right now, I choose to turn away from sin, and I ask You to cleanse me of all unrighteousness. I believe that Your Son, Jesus, died on the cross to take away my sins. I also believe that He rose again from the dead so that I may be justified and made righteous through faith in Him. I call upon the name of Jesus Christ to be the Savior and Lord of my life. Jesus, I choose to follow You, and I ask that You fill me with the power of the Holy Spirit. I declare right now that I am a born-again child of God. I am free from sin, and full of the right-eousness of God. I am saved in Jesus' name, amen.

If you have prayed this prayer to receive Jesus Christ as your Savior, or if this book has changed your life, we would like to hear from you. Please write us at:

Harrison House Publishers

P.O. Box 35035

Tulsa, Oklahoma 74153

You can also visit us on the Web at

www.harrisonhouse.com

Additional copies of this book
are available from your local bookstore.